I0880109

AMERICA'S STORY

Historical Sources on World War I

CHET'LA SEBREE AND ADRIANE RUGGIERO

Cavendish Square
New York

Published in 2020 by Cavendish Square Publishing, LLC
243 5th Avenue, Suite 136, New York, NY 10016

First Edition

Website: cavendishsq.com

Library of Congress Cataloging-in-Publication Data

Names: Sebree, Chet'la, author. | Ruggiero, Adriane, author.
Title: Historical sources on World War I / Chet'la Sebree, Adriane Ruggiero.
Other titles: Historical sources on World War One
Description: First edition. | New York : Cavendish Square Publishing, 2020. | Series: America's story | Includes index. | Audience: Ages 13 | Audience: Grades 7-9 | Summary: "Although World War I started in summer 1914 after the assassination of Archduke Franz Ferdinand, the United States didn't enter the war until April 1917. In this book, students will learn about the United States' initial decision to remain neutral, the cost of said decision, and the effects of the war both abroad and at home, while hearing directly from the men and women, soldiers and civilians, and politicians and doctors involved in the conflict. Through this cross-section of individuals, students will come to understand how the Great War not only changed the face of Europe but changed America and the nature of international warfare"-- Provided by publisher.
Identifiers: LCCN 2019028561 (print) | LCCN 2019028562 (ebook) | ISBN 9781502652201 (library binding) | ISBN 9781502652195 (paperback) | ISBN 9781502652218 (ebook)
Subjects: LCSH: World War, 1914-1918--Sources--Juvenile literature.
Classification: LCC D522.7 .S39 2020 (print) | LCC D522.7 (ebook) | DDC 940.3--dc23
LC record available at https://lccn.loc.gov/2019028561
LC ebook record available at https://lccn.loc.gov/2019028562

Copy Editor: Nathan Heidelberger
Associate Art Director: Alan Sliwinski
Designer: Christina Shults
Production Coordinator: Karol Szymczuk
Photo Research: J8 Media

The photographs in this book are used by permission and through the courtesy of: Cover Heritage Images/Hulton Archive/Getty Images, (background and used throughout) Foxstudio/Shutterstock.com; p. 4 US Army Signal Corps/American Stock/Getty Images; p. 8 Mondadori Portfolio/Getty Images; p. 11 Wikimedia Commons/File:Map 1914 WWI Alliances.jpg/Public Domain; pp. 14, 31 Culture Club/Getty Images; p. 20 The Print Collector/Getty Images; p. 25 DeAgostini/Getty Images; p. 34 Wikimedia Commons/National Museum of the U.S. Navy/File:Periscope in a German U-Boat submarine observes a battle, WWI (33102861221).jpg/Public Domain; p. 39 Photo 12/Universal Images Group/Getty Images; p. 48 Galerie Bilderwelt/Getty Images; p. 53 US Government/Wikimedia Commons/File:Al capone draftcard.jpg/Public Domain; p. 56 Everett Collection/Alamy Stock Photo; p. 58 DEA/Biblioteca Ambrosiana/Getty Images; p. 65 Paul Thompson/War Department/National Archives/The LIFE Picture Collection/Getty Images; p. 68 National Archives/Wikimedia Commons/File:Private Ed Williams with French Croix de Guerre of the 369th Infantry Regiment (United States) (cropped).jpg/Public Domain; pp. 70, 109 Hulton Archive/Getty Images; pp. 76, 79, 116, 125 Bettmann/Getty Images; pp. 82, 91 Corbis/Getty Images; p. 88 Wikimedia Commons/File:HarveyCushing.JPG/Public Domain; p. 94 Swim Ink 2, LLC/Corbis/Getty Images; p. 97 Chicago History Museum/Getty Images; p. 102 Library of Congress/Corbis/VCG/Getty Images; p. 104 Glenn Harper/Alamy Stock Photo.

Printed in the United States of America

AMERICA'S STORY

CONTENTS

Primary sources like this image of US soldiers in the Argonne Forest in northeastern France give us a glimpse of what World War I was like for the people who fought in it.

Primary Sources

In the pages that follow, you'll hear from many different people from a time in America's past. These selections will vary in length. Some are long, and others are short. You'll find many easy to understand at first reading, but some may require several readings. All the selections have one thing in common, however. They are primary sources. They are important to us because they are the core material for all historical investigation.

What Is a Primary Source?

The term "primary source" is the name historians give to the information that makes up the record of human existence. A primary source is "history" itself. Primary sources are evidence. They give historians the all-important clues they need to understand the past.

Perhaps you have read a detective story in which an investigator has to solve a mystery by piecing together bits of evidence that he or she uncovers. The detective makes deductions, or educated guesses based on the evidence, and solves the mystery once all the deductions point in a certain direction. Historians work in much the same way. Like detectives, they analyze data through careful reading and rereading. After much analysis, they draw conclusions about an event, a person, or an entire era. Different historians may analyze the same evidence and come to different conclusions. That is why there is often strong disagreement about an event.

Primary sources are sometimes called documents. It is a rather dry word to describe what can be just about anything: an official speech by a government leader, an old map, an act of Congress, a letter, a diary entry, a newspaper article, a song, a poster, or even a cartoon.

By examining the following primary sources, you, the reader, will be taking on the role of historian. Here is your chance to jump into a specific moment in time: World War I. You'll come to know the voices of the men and women who lived during those years when America took part in its first global war. You'll read the words they wrote to express their thoughts about what was happening around them.

How to Read a Primary Source

Each document in this book deals with events surrounding the war and the involvement of the United States in it. Some of the documents are from government archives or from the official papers of major historical figures. Others are taken from the letters ordinary people wrote or from the newspapers that kept Americans informed. All of these documents help us to understand what it was like to live in the years when Americans sacrificed their time, resources, and lives for an international cause.

As you read each document, ask yourself some basic questions. Who is writing or speaking? Who is that person's intended audience? What is he or she trying to tell the audience? Is the message clearly expressed, or is it implied, or stated indirectly? What words does the writer use to convey his or her message? Are the words emotional or neutral in tone? These are questions that can help you think critically about a primary source.

There are also some tools in each chapter to help you unpack these documents. Some terms and concepts you may not be familiar with have been explained in sidebars. Also, questions follow each of the documents to help you focus and think through the primary source you have just read. As you read each selection, you'll probably come up with many questions of your own. That's great! The work of a historian always leads to many, many questions. Some can be easily answered, while others will require more investigation.

Although tensions existed throughout Europe in the early twentieth century, the assassination of Archduke Franz Ferdinand, heir to the Austro-Hungarian Empire, sparked World War I.

INTRODUCTION

The First World War

The First World War (1914–1918) is called a world war because it was fought on several continents. Although most of the fighting took place in Europe, the conflict was also carried out in the Middle East and in Africa. The First World War—also known as World War I—was also the first major war of the twentieth century. During the war, the most powerful nations in Europe formed two alliances. One group, known as the Allies, consisted of France, Russia, and Great Britain. Later, Italy and the United States would join the Allies, as would other, smaller European nations. On the other side of the war were the Central Powers, including Germany, Austria-Hungary, and the Ottoman Empire, which was made up of countries in southeastern Europe and the Middle East. Throughout the war, other nations across the world, like Japan, New Zealand, and Australia, would join the fight.

Europe at the Turn of the Century

Tension existed in Europe before the start of World War I. In the early 1900s, Great Britain and Germany were in a race for control of the seas. Both nations started massive shipbuilding programs. The ships were fitted with huge guns capable of blowing any other ship out of the water. The race for sea power increased tensions between these two major powers.

Other factors also increased the unease. France was a longtime rival of Germany. It feared German military power. The French expected Great Britain, an ally, to fight Germany if that nation invaded neutral Belgium, France's neighbor. None of these tensions actually started the war, however. The immediate cause lay to the southeast, in the Balkans. This region, partly ruled by Austria-Hungary, was a powder keg that, once lit, would blow apart all of Europe.

Declarations of War and Neutrality

In 1908, Austria-Hungary annexed Bosnia and Herzegovina, a region of the Balkans. This means that Austria-Hungary incorporated Bosnia and Herzegovina into its country. This action angered another Balkan state, Serbia, whose ally was Russia. Many Serbs lived in the annexed territory.

Both Austria-Hungary and Russia saw the Balkans as a place to advance their long-range plans. Austria-Hungary hoped to extend the borders of its empire south to the Dardanelles, the narrow body of water that connects the Aegean and Black Seas. Russia had long wanted control of the Dardanelles because it was a warm-water route for Russian trade. For its part, Serbia wanted to enfold Bosnia and other Slavic states into an enlarged Serbia. Such an action was likely to anger Austria-Hungary.

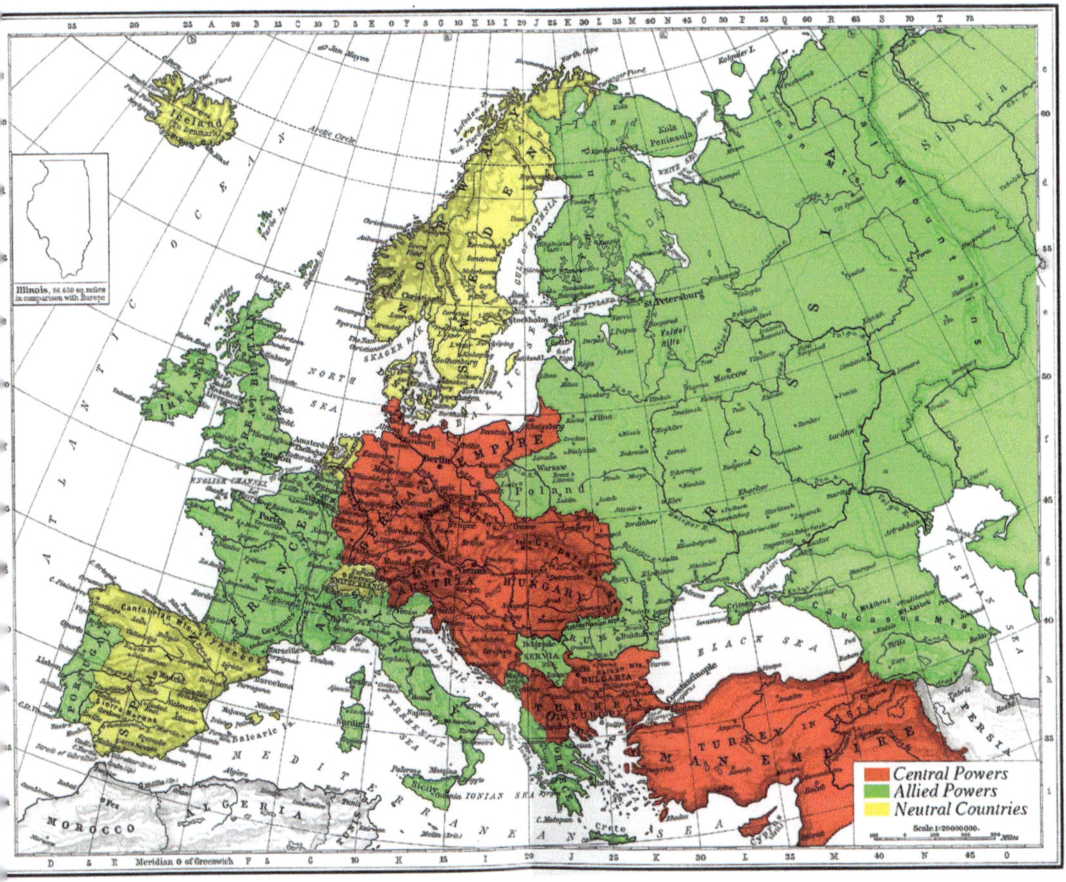

Although some countries remained neutral (*yellow*), many European nations joined World War I on the side of the Central Powers (*red*) or Allied powers (*green*). The United States was neutral until 1917, when it joined the Allies.

Tensions in the region were great, but war was still avoidable. That all changed on June 28, 1914. That morning, Archduke Franz Ferdinand of Austria-Hungary was assassinated by a Bosnian Serb nationalist in Sarajevo, the capital of Bosnia. The archduke was the prince of the Austro-Hungarian Empire.

This caused the representatives of each nation to send ultimatums, or demands, to each other. The ruler of Germany, Kaiser Wilhelm II, immediately promised to come to the aid of Austria-Hungary if it decided to punish Serbia. When Serbia received the Austrian ultimatum, it began to mobilize, or prepare for war. Meanwhile, Great Britain tried to keep the peace. On July 28, Austria-Hungary declared war on Serbia. Days later, Russia began to prepare for war, and soon, Germany and Russia were at war. Germany followed by mobilizing on its border with France, so France began to mobilize on its border with Germany.

Great Britain had to decide what to do. Would the British stand behind their allies—France and Russia—or remain neutral? The deciding factor was whether Germany would respect the neutrality of Belgium, a small country that stood between Germany and France.

Italy declared itself neutral early on. However, this neutrality would only last a short while. In the spring of 1915, Italy declared war on its former ally, Austria-Hungary. It made this decision because Italy believed that the Allies were winning the war. If the Allies won the war, Italy was hopeful about the possibility of picking up more territory.

While the leaders of the European powers promised their soldiers that the war would be short, the American president had other concerns. President Woodrow Wilson urged Americans (many of whom were of German ancestry or even recent immigrants from Germany) not to take sides. He also proclaimed that the United States would remain neutral, and it did so until 1917.

Military Strategy

Germany's generals had a grand plan. They wanted to quickly invade France to the west, knock it out of the war, and then turn their army on Russia to the east. The quickest route to northern

France, however, was through low-lying Belgium. Years earlier, Germany—along with Great Britain and the other countries—had agreed to respect Belgium's neutral status. Now, Germany demanded that its army be allowed to march through Belgium. Great Britain rejected the demand and asked that Germany stop its plans to invade. When the German leaders refused and declared war on France while invading Belgium, Great Britain declared war on Germany. The date was August 4, 1914.

Germany's invasion of Belgium and rapid advance on France caught the Allies by surprise. German forces moved in on Paris, and the French army fell back in retreat. Then, in September, the French saw an opportunity to attack the German advance. In several fierce battles, beginning with the Battle of the Marne, French and German armies battled each other to a draw. The German plan to crush the French in a single hammer blow failed. However, neither side was able to completely defeat the other. By the end of the year, German and Allied troops had dug themselves in along France's northern boundary.

To escape bombardment by the enemy's heavy guns, each army constructed a series of trenches that snaked back and forth for about 400 miles (644 kilometers) from the North Sea south through western Belgium and then across France to the border of Switzerland. This became known as the Western Front. It was impossible to go around the system of trenches. The only tactic was for an army to make a complete frontal assault against the dug-in enemy.

Both forces used this tactic to try to break through the other's defenses. The results were terrible. Millions of soldiers were killed by machine-gun fire or exploding shells as they scrambled out of their protective trenches and moved across open fields. Hidden explosives and barbed wire made the contested territory a "no-man's-land." The war settled into a stalemate. Neither side was able to knock its enemy out of the fight.

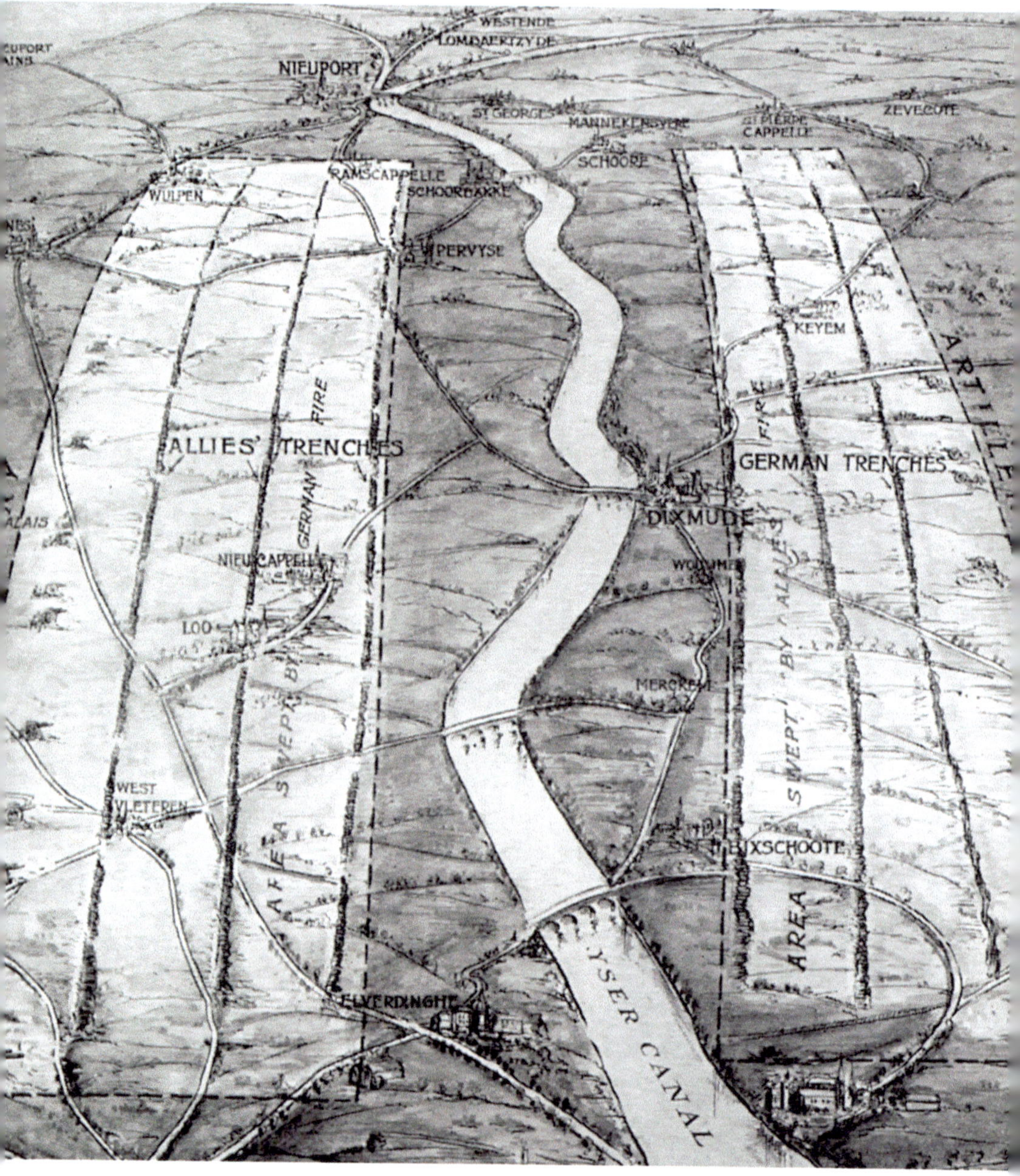

Trench warfare was a key component to the war fought on the Western Front in France. In between the trenches was a dangerous expanse known as "no-man's-land."

On the Eastern Front, poorly prepared Russian soldiers were massacred as they attacked German forces across open fields. In Turkey, Australian and New Zealander soldiers of the Allied force unsuccessfully fought the Turks for control of the Dardanelles and access to the Black Sea.

Strategies at Sea

At sea, Great Britain was using its navy to blockade, or cut off, all shipments of food and war supplies to Germany. In response, Germany declared a sea war against British and Allied ships. Germans also targeted ships of neutral nations, as they suspected these ships were secretly carrying supplies for the Allies. On these ships, Germany used its most powerful weapon in the water: the submarine.

When submarines harassed American merchant ships, Americans began to call for a response. On May 7, 1915, a German submarine sank a British passenger ship called the *Lusitania*. One hundred and twenty-eight Americans lost their lives. Despite public outrage over the *Lusitania* tragedy, President Wilson was determined to keep America neutral. In the election of 1916, he ran for reelection with the slogan "He kept us out of war." He won.

Nonetheless, the year 1917 saw America's entry into World War I. In January, President Wilson called for "peace without victory" in a speech before the United States Senate. A few days later, the German kaiser, or ruler, called for unrestricted submarine warfare. This announcement spurred President Wilson to cut off all relations with Germany. This was a step just short of a declaration of war.

In the same month, the British informed Wilson of the contents of the infamous Zimmermann telegram. The note revealed a German plot to involve Mexico in a war against the United States. Furious, Americans called for war. In March, German submarines torpedoed three American ships. Wilson knew that any chance of keeping the nation out of the war had been lost. On April 2,

1917, he asked Congress to declare war against Germany. Four days later, the United States was at war.

US Involvement

The American Expeditionary Force (AEF) was the name given to the American forces in World War I. Its leader was General John J. Pershing. The first American troops arrived in France on June 24, 1917, and they paraded in the streets of Paris ten days later. The Americans arrived at the time when the French forces were at their lowest point. Exhausted by years of trench warfare, French soldiers refused to attack the enemy. British troops were equally worn-out. In contrast, the Americans were fresh and ready to fight. Soon, they were tested in battle.

In June 1918, German forces smashed through the Allied lines on the Western Front and threatened to seize Paris. Doughboys, a nickname for US Army soldiers, and Marines were rushed forward to stop the advance. They met German forces near Belleau Wood. The Marines, whom the Germans nicknamed "Devil Dogs," boldly vowed to hold the ground at all cost. And they did just that. After the battle was over, the German advance had been checked. Americans had earned the admiration of friend and foe alike.

Other key battles followed. The Americans held their ground at Château-Thierry and attacked at Saint-Mihiel. In the rugged Argonne Forest, American soldiers clawed and crawled through a wilderness studded with German machine-gun nests. The doughboys called the area the "meatgrinder." The outnumbered Americans fought off the Germans and eventually drove them from the Argonne.

Waving a White Flag

The spirit of American soldiers in combat proved to Germany that the war would continue for some time. Eventually, the Americans would overwhelm Germany's weary army. In early October 1918, the German leaders requested an armistice, or truce. This would end to fighting on land, by sea, and in the air. Kaiser Wilhelm II faced rising discontent by Germans and the collapse of his armies. Eventually, he abdicated, or gave up, the throne.

Meanwhile the Allies were closing in on all fronts. In the Middle East, the British were on the verge of defeating the Ottoman Turks, an ally of Germany. On the Western Front, the British, French, and Americans were smashing through German lines. On November 10, a republic was declared in Germany. This meant that the country was no longer a monarchy but a country ruled by the people through elected representatives, like the United States. One day later, on November 11, the Germans signed the armistice in a railway car in a forest outside of Paris. The Great War, as World War I is often called, had come to an end.

The Human Toll

What had the war accomplished? Four empires—the German, Austro-Hungarian, Russian, and Ottoman—ceased to be. Great Britain had lost about 1 million men; France, 1.3 million; Germany, 1.7 million; Russia, 1.7 million; and Austria-Hungary, 1.2 million. American losses—about 115,000—were small in comparison but large for the short period of time the AEF was in combat. One writer estimated that more men died in a week's fighting in the

Argonne Forest than in the entire American Revolution. In addition to the huge number of dead, many soldiers were prisoners or missing. Others returned home without legs or arms. Those who had been gassed never recovered their health. Others were mentally wounded, victims of shell shock or battle fatigue—terms that describe what we know today to be post-traumatic stress disorder (PTSD). To add to the already terrible losses of the war, a worldwide outbreak of influenza in 1918 killed between 20 million and 40 million people. The most vulnerable were young men and women—the very persons most involved in fighting and supporting the war.

The Aftermath

When the delegates of the Allies met in Versailles, France, in 1919 to discuss the terms of peace, they were a divided group. One year earlier, President Wilson had presented his plan for world peace called the Fourteen Points. Some of the points he proposed included a reduction in the number of war weapons a nation could have and the right of all nations to govern themselves. He also wanted to establish an international organization, which he called the League of Nations. The organization's responsibility would be to keep international peace and prevent future wars.

However, at Versailles, Britain and France were more interested in punishing Germany. When the peace treaty was signed in June of that year, Germany lost all of its overseas possessions and some of its territory. The treaty also required Germany to reduce its once-mighty army to one hundred thousand men. Most severe of all, Germany was forced to pay for all of the civilian damage caused during the war. The reaction in Germany was one of outrage. In time, resentment over the harsh terms of the peace treaty, coupled with economic hardship, would give rise to extremist political groups. By the 1930s, these new political groups would lead Germany into another war: World War II.

In the United States, people were happy to see the return of peace after World War I. Many said that the country should never again become involved in the affairs of other nations. They preached this philosophy of isolationism despite President Wilson's plea that the United States not turn its back on world affairs. In Congress, opponents of the president rejected his idea for the League of Nations. They also refused to sign the Treaty of Versailles. When Wilson left office in 1921, his health was ruined and his ideas about building a new world were largely cast aside. Nevertheless, the United States emerged from the war as a world leader.

THE DAILY MAIL, WEDNESDAY, AUGUST 5, 1914.

GREAT BRITAI DECLARES WA ON GERMANY.

SUMMARY REJECTION O BRITISH ULTIMATUM.

The following announcement was issued at the Foreig Office at 12.15 a.m.:—

"Owing to the summary rejection by the German Govern ment of the request made by His Majesty's Government fo assurances that the neutrality of Belgium would be respecte His Majesty's Ambassador in Berlin has received his passport and His Majesty's Government has declared to the Germa Government that a state of war exists between Great Britai and Germany as from 11 p.m. on August 4."

Huge [illegible] Trafalgar Square greete the news with round after round of cheers.

11 p.m. London time is midnight Berlin time, the hour a which the British ultimatum expired.

Newspapers were central to people on the home front and abroad learning about the war.

1

Early News of the War Abroad

World War I broke out in the summer of 1914 after months of simmering tensions among major European powers. No one thought the war would last for long. National leaders hoped to achieve victories in time to bring the soldiers home by Christmas. It was not to be. The war did not end by Christmas of 1914. Instead, it dragged on for four long years. The way the war would unfold would surprise many.

A New Type of Warfare

During most of that time, soldiers lined up in trenches that stretched across the landscape of northern France all the way south to the Swiss border. There they sat and waited for their commander's order to advance against the opposing army's lines. These attacks turned out to be mass slaughters as men marched into a rain of bullets and the explosions of thousands of shells. The rain of bullets, which came from machine guns, was new to many. Developed during the 1880s and 1890s, these guns could fire six hundred bullets per minute from 1,000 yards (900 meters) away. This meant that as men emerged from trenches to attack, they were quickly brought down by the rapidly firing guns.

Machine guns weren't the only relatively new technology. Poison gas was a new weapon as well. It was not only effective at disabling soldiers during warfare but also caused long-term suffering among survivors. This was like nothing anyone had ever experienced before. Americans would quickly learn about the devastation this new type of warfare was causing.

A Word of Warning

Americans kept informed of events abroad primarily through newspaper articles and the numerous accounts of correspondents reporting from overseas. For instance, President Woodrow Wilson's closest adviser during this time was Colonel Edward House. Colonel House traveled to Europe in the spring of 1914 to observe the tensions between the major European powers.

The following excerpt is from House's letter to Wilson. It was written in May of 1914. The outbreak of war was just a few months away, brought about in part by the competition among the major powers to build bigger and better-armed armies and navies.

> The situation is extraordinary. It is militarism run stark mad. Unless someone acting for you can bring about a different understanding, there is some day to be an awful cataclysm. No one in Europe can do it. There is too much hatred, too many jealousies. Whenever England consents, France and Russia will close in on Germany and Austria. England does not want Germany wholly crushed, for she would then

have to reckon alone with her ancient enemy, Russia. But if Germany insists upon an ever increasing navy, then England will have no choice. The best chance for peace is an understanding between England and Germany in regard to naval armaments and yet there is some disadvantage to us by these two getting too close.

—From Charles Seymour, ed., *The Intimate Papers of Colonel House* (Boston and New York: Houghton Mifflin, 1926).

CONSIDER THIS

1. Why, in House's opinion, was it impossible for the nations of Europe to stop militarism?
2. What does Colonel House mean by an "understanding" between England and Germany?

A Conspirator's Account of the Assassination

Archduke Franz Ferdinand was the nephew of the emperor of Austria-Hungary. He was also heir to the Austro-Hungarian throne, meaning one day he would rule the empire. However, he was assassinated in the Bosnian city of Sarajevo on June 28, 1914. The assassin was a Bosnian Serb nationalist named Gavrilo Princip. This event was the spark that ignited World War I.

The following is an account of the killing as witnessed by one of Princip's fellow terrorists, Borijove Jevtic. Both Princip and Jevtic were members of a secret society devoted to Serbian independence. Jevtic's account appeared in numerous newspapers, including the *New York World*.

KEY TERMS AND CONCEPTS

From Colonel Edward House's letter:
armament Military weapons or equipment.
cataclysm A large-scale and violent event.
consent To give permission.
reckon To deal with.
stark mad Completely crazy.

From Borijove Jevtic's account:
conspirator A person involved in a conspiracy, or a secret plan to do something unlawful or harmful.
feasible Possible or easy to do.
Gabrinovic Nedeljko Čabrinović was another one of the conspirators who worked to assassinate Archduke Franz Ferdinand.
retinue A group of people who accompany an important person.

When Francis Ferdinand and his retinue drove from the [train] station they were allowed to pass the first two conspirators. The motor cars were driving too fast to make an attempt feasible and in the crowd were many Serbians; throwing a grenade would have killed many innocent people. When the car passed Gabrinovic … he threw his grenade. It hit the side of the car, but Francis Ferdinand threw himself back and was uninjured. Several officers riding in his attendance were injured. The cars sped to the

Archduke Franz Ferdinand (*center*) and Sophie, Duchess of Hohenberg (*right*), were assassinated on June 28, 1914. Sophie was a woman of lesser nobility whom the archduke loved and fought the government to marry.

Town Hall and the rest of the conspirators did not interfere with them. After the reception in the Town Hall General Potiorek, the Austrian Commander, pleaded with Francis Ferdinand to leave the city, as it was seething with rebellion. The Archduke was persuaded to drive the shortest way out of the city and to go quickly. The road to the maneuvers [an army practice to be witnessed by the Archduke] was shaped like the letter V, making a sharp turn at the bridge over the River Milgacka. Francis Ferdinand's car could go fast enough until it reached this spot but here it was forced to slow down for the turn. Here Princip had taken his stand.

As the car came abreast he stepped forward from the curb, drew his automatic pistol from his coat and fired two shots. The first struck the wife of the Archduke, the Archduchess Sofia, in the abdomen. She was an expectant mother. She died instantly. The second bullet struck the Archduke close to the heart. He uttered only one word, "Sofia"—a call to his stricken wife. Then his head fell back and he collapsed. He died almost instantly. The officers seized Princip. They beat him over the head with the flat of their swords. They knocked him down, they kicked him ... all but killed him. The next day they put chains on Princip's feet, which he wore till his death.

—From the *New York World*, June 29, 1914.

CONSIDER THIS

1. How does this newspaper account answer the questions who, what, where, when, and why?
2. After reading this account, do you think the assassination of Franz Ferdinand could have been prevented? Why?

A Dispatch from Belgium

Richard Harding Davis was a famous American war correspondent. Wherever there was a conflict, Davis was there to tell the story. Davis began his career in 1886 as a reporter for the *Philadelphia Record*. During the Spanish-American War, he rode with Theodore Roosevelt and his Rough Riders. His vivid writing style brought him many assignments, but he was not limited to reporting the news. Davis was also a noted author of short stories and novels.

With the outbreak of war in August 1914, Davis was in Belgium, where he witnessed the German invasion of the neutral nation. The following excerpt is from Davis's eyewitness account of the German entrance into Brussels, the Belgian capital. In journalism, these accounts are called dispatches.

> At the sight of the first few regiments of the enemy we were thrilled with interest. After for three hours they had passed in one unbroken steel-gray column we were bored. But when hour after hour passed and there was no halt, no breathing time … the thing became uncanny, inhuman. It held the mystery and menace of fog rolling toward you across the sea.
>
> The gray of the uniforms worn by both officers and men helped this air of mystery. Only the sharpest eye could detect among the thousands that passed the slightest difference. All moved under a cloak of invisibility. That it [the color gray] was selected to clothe and disguise the German when he fights is typical of the German staff in striving for efficiency to leave nothing to chance, to neglect no detail. After you have seen this … uniform … you are convinced that for the German soldier it is his strongest weapon. Even the most expert marksman cannot hit a target

he cannot see. It is a gray green. ... the gray of the hour just before daybreak, the gray of unpolished steel, of mist among green trees. In comparison the yellow khaki of our own American army is about as invisible as the [red and gold] flag of Spain.

I have followed in campaigns six armies, but excepting not even our own, the Japanese, or the British, I have not seen one so thoroughly equipped. I am not speaking of the fighting qualities of any army, only of the equipment and organization. The German army moved into this city as smoothly and as compactly as an Empire State Express.

The infantry came in files of five, two hundred men to each company; the Lancers in columns of four with not a pennant missing. The quick firing guns and fieldpieces were an hour at a time in passing ... The men of the infantry sang "Fatherland, My Fatherland." Between each line of song they took three steps. At times two thousand men were singing together in absolute rhythm and beat. When the melody gave way the silence was broken only by the stamp of iron-shod boots, and then again the song rose. For seven hours the army passed in such solid columns that not once might a taxicab or trolley car pass through the city. Like a river of steel it flowed, gray and ghostlike.

—From Richard Harding Davis, dispatch to the *News Chronicle*, London, August 23, 1914.

KEY TERMS AND CONCEPTS

From Richard Harding Davis's *News Chronicle* dispatch:

campaign A series of connected military operations.

compactly Tightly or orderly.

company A military unit.

Empire State Express A passenger train in the United States.

fieldpiece A gun used on the battlefield.

infantry Foot soldiers.

iron-shod boots Steel-toed boots.

Lancers Members of a military unit who carried lances, or steel-tipped spears.

marksman A person who is skilled at shooting a specific target.

menace Threat or danger.

pennant A flag or banner.

regiment A military unit.

uncanny Abnormal or unexpected, particularly something mysterious or supernatural.

From Richard Harding Davis's *New York Tribune* dispatch:

Burgomaster The mayor.

concentration camp A place in which a large number of people, such as prisoners of war, refugees, or religious minorities, are detained, or kept against their will, by military personnel or armed guards.

Hotel de Ville City hall.

veldt Grasslands.

CONSIDER THIS

1. How did Davis use words to paint a picture of the event he described?
2. What was Davis's impression of the German army?
3. In your view, what impact would this dispatch have had on readers in America?

A Description of the Burning of a Belgian City

Richard Harding Davis continued to report from German-occupied Belgium. In the following excerpt from a dispatch he filed in August 1914, Davis describes how the Germans set fire to Louvain, a city in Belgium. The Germans did this as punishment. They believed they'd been fired upon by Belgian snipers, or people who shoot from a hiding place. Davis's story helped build support for the war among Americans despite the fact that President Wilson had declared the United States neutral.

> London, August 30—I left Brussels on Thursday afternoon and have just arrived in London. For two hours on Thursday night I was in what for six hundred years has been the city of Louvain. The Germans were burning it, and to hide their work kept us locked in the railroad carriages. But the story was written against the sky ... and we could read it in the faces of women and children being led to concentration camps and of citizens on their way to be shot.
>
> The reason ... as given to me on Thursday morning by General von Lutwitz, military governor of Brussels, was this: on Wednesday while the German military

The destruction of Louvain was one of a series of atrocities committed by the Germans in the early days of the war. Their sweep through Belgium would leave six thousand civilians dead and twenty-five thousand houses destroyed.

commander of the troops of Louvain was at the Hotel de Ville talking to the Burgomaster, a son of the Burgomaster with an automatic pistol shot the chief of staff and German staff surgeons. Lutwitz claims this was the signal for the civil guard, in civilian clothes on roofs, to fire upon the German soldiers in the open square below. Fifty Germans were killed ... For that, said Lutwitz, Louvain must be wiped out. "The Hotel de Ville," he added, "was a beautiful building; it is a pity it must be destroyed."

The city dates from the eleventh century, and the population was 42,000. The citizens were brewers, lacemakers, and manufacturers of ornaments for churches.

When by troop train we reached Louvain, the entire heart of the city was destroyed and fire had reached the Boulevard Tirlemont, which faces the railroad station. The night was windless, and the sparks rose in steady … pillars. In their work the soldiers were moving from the heart of the city to the outskirts, street by street, from house to house. In each building, so German soldiers told me, they began at the first floor, and when that was burning steadily passed to the one next. There were no exceptions—whether it was a store, chapel, or private residence it was destroyed … In each deserted shop or house the furniture was piled, the torch was struck under it, and into the air went the savings of years, souvenirs of children, of parents, heirlooms that had passed from generation to generation.

The people had time only to fill a pillowcase and fly. Some were not so fortunate, and by thousands, like flocks of sheep, they were rounded up and marched through the night to concentration camps.

In other wars I have watched men on one hilltop … fire at men on another hill. … But in those fights there were no women and children, and the shells struck only vacant stretches of veldt or uninhabited mountainsides. At Louvain it was war upon the defenseless.

—From Richard Harding Davis, dispatch to the *New York Tribune*, August 31, 1914.

CONSIDER THIS

1. In Davis's mind, what was the worst thing that happened at Louvain?
2. How do you think Davis got the information to write his dispatch?
3. What is the tone of Davis's writing in this selection? What do you think his intention was?

The Impact of Early Reports

Dispatches like Richard Harding Davis's brought the war to American newspapers, which brought the reality of the war into people's daily lives. Even though the war was happening an ocean away, there was no escaping it.

Even still, President Woodrow Wilson tried desperately to keep the United States out of World War I. He knew the terrible cost the war would have on his fellow citizens. In an attempt to stop the conflict, Wilson asked the nations at war to state their aims, but neither side would do so.

Many Americans shared the president's hesitance to get involved. As they tried to understand the confusing causes leading up to the war, Americans became uneasy about foreign affairs. Some citizens in the United States had no sympathy for the nations at war. Critics of the war thought it was just an opportunity for weapons merchants and bankers to make money from the suffering of others. Other Americans disagreed about which side of the war should be supported.

The end of American neutrality in World War I was partly brought about by German attacks on American ships.

2 The End of American Neutrality

For many Americans, World War I posed special problems. For instance, many Americans had divided loyalties. In 1917, America had a large immigrant population. One out of every three Americans was foreign born or had a foreign-born parent. Would these new Americans fight for their native lands or for their adopted country?

Support Without Military Action

In due time, each aggressive action by Germany filled many Americans with growing outrage. They supported the victims of the war and wanted to help them. France was an American ally and the main power on the continent of Europe fighting against Germany. It needed money and reinforcements for its battle-weary soldiers. Great Britain, France's ally, also needed loans and help in the form of food and war materials. The United States could not turn its back on their pleas.

Even still, the United States found ways of supporting the war without directly being involved. Americans sent supplies and money to support the troops abroad. However, the war at sea made it impossible for Americans to remain neutral during the war.

Submarines End American Neutrality

Germany engaged in submarine warfare against all ships around the British Isles. This included neutral ships in the war zone. Ships of neutral nations such as the United States were stopped and searched for food or anything else that might help the enemy. Germany went so far as to even attack all ships in the war zone, including American ships. This eventually swept American neutrality aside.

As more American lives were lost, citizens realized the impossibility of staying out of the fight. In 1917, Woodrow Wilson asked for a declaration of war between the United States and Germany and its allies. In a short time, American soldiers were at the front.

Danger on the High Seas

When the war broke out in 1914, Great Britain tried to starve Germany into defeat by blocking off German ports. Great Britain was the world's leading sea power at the time. Unable to block Britain's ports with its ships, Germany took another kind of action. It used submarines to wage war on its enemies.

German submarines were called U-boats, short for *unterseeboote*. They marked the introduction of a new kind of warfare. Ships could be blown out of the water by torpedoes fired by an invisible enemy. In February 1915, Germany began unrestricted submarine warfare. It announced that waters around the British Isles were a war zone. Any neutral ships were exposed to danger if they entered the zone.

A submarine commander, Lieutenant Otto Weddigen, wrote the following account of an attack by his U-boat. During the course of one hour, the U-boat attacked and sank three large British warships called cruisers.

> It was ten minutes after 6 on the morning of last Tuesday when I caught sight of one of the big cruisers of the enemy. I was then eighteen sea miles northwest of the Hook of Holland. I had then traveled considerably more than 200 miles from my base … I had been going ahead partly submerged, with about five feet of my periscope showing. Almost immediately I caught sight of the first cruiser and two others. I submerged completely and laid my course so as to bring up in the center of the trio, which held a sort of triangular formation. I could see their gray-black sides riding high over the water.
>
> When I first sighted them they were near enough for torpedo work, but I wanted to make my aim sure, so I went down and in on them. I had taken the position of the three ships before submerging, and I succeeded in getting another flash through my periscope before I began action. I soon reached what I regarded as a good shooting point.
>
> Then I loosed one of my torpedoes at the middle ship. I was then about twelve feet under water, and got the shot off in good shape … I climbed to the surface to get a sight … and discovered that the shot had gone straight and true, striking the ship, which I later learned was the *Aboukir* …

There were a fountain of water, a burst of smoke, a flash of fire, and part of the cruiser rose in the air. Then I heard a roar and felt reverberations sent through the water by the detonation. She had been broken apart, and sank in a few minutes.

—From Lieutenant Otto Weddigen, Commander of the U-9, "The First Submarine Blow Is Struck," reprinted in *New York Times Current History: The European War, Volume 2* (New York: The New York Times Co., 1915).

CONSIDER THIS

1. What skills did the U-boat commander use to destroy the enemy ships?
2. Soldiers and sailors have to report their actions to their commanders after an engagement like the one described here. What is the purpose of these reports?
3. Put yourself in the role of a sailor aboard a British or neutral ship. How would you feel about sailing into a war zone?

Torpedoes Strike

Lieutenant Weddigen's account was just one of many accounts of torpedo attacks. On May 7, 1915, the British passenger liner *Lusitania* was torpedoed by a German submarine while traveling from New York to Liverpool, England. Although unarmed, the *Lusitania* was carrying cases of rifle ammunition and other war goods. These goods were apparently destined for the Allied armies. Around 1,200 passengers and crew died when the ship sank off the coast of Ireland. Among the dead were 128 Americans. In the

Approximately 1,200 of the nearly 2,000 passengers died when the *Lusitania* was attacked and sunk.

United States and Great Britain, the public reacted with outrage as newspapers told the grim story. Other submarine attacks followed. Ship travel across the Atlantic became more and more dangerous.

The following excerpt describes the torpedoing of a British ship. It was written by Albert Kinross, an officer on board.

> The first torpedo struck us at a few minutes past ten o'clock in the morning. I was down below in the saloon with E. We had both kept a boat-watch during the night and were the last officers to come to breakfast. When the torpedo struck, there was no mistaking it for anything else. E and I laughed, as much to say: "Here she is!" Then I put on my cork belt ... and leaped up the three flights of stairs that led to the liner's deck and my own boat station. E raced with me. I have never seen him since. The stewards and cooks raced with us too. There was something theatrical about that picture—so many

white jackets and blue uniform trousers and white overalls. All this time—it might have been a couple of minutes—the greater part of me was so active that I have no recollection of any instant devoted to fear.

As one rushed upstairs one thought of things one had valued yesterday—two brand-new pairs of boots, one's field glasses, some money—they seemed now so utterly of no account. Providence must have been with me, for having arrived on deck, I stood flush before my boat, Number 13. I stood there and took charge. To [the] left of me the right people were busy with our sixty-six sisters. These ladies were part of the staff of a new hospital unit. Safely they were put into their boats, safely lowered, and safely rowed away from us. We cheered them as they left, and they cheered back.

I had filled my boat as full as it would go. All was ready. I stepped on board and gave the signal. Then slowly we descended. Above our heads one of the ship's officers was seeing to it that we went down all right. Immediately below us was another boat. It pushed off at last, and now we were free to hit the water. Before we pushed off I took on five of the crew who had helped to lower us. They swarmed down the ropes and reached us safely. Then I refused to take anybody else and we got oars and rowed away. Only then did I notice that the ship had stopped dead.

The big ship—she was near to 15,000 tons—stood like an island, and as if she could stand forever. Then ... there was a flash and an explosion. A second torpedo had struck ... We noticed now that she had

KEY TERMS AND CONCEPTS

From Albert Kinross's account:

bow The curved, front part of a ship.

list A tilt to one side.

starboard The right side of a ship.

stern The rear part of a boat.

From Woodrow Wilson's speech:

strife Bitter or violent conflict.

a definite list to starboard. The angle grew steeper, and then suddenly her bow dropped, her stern lifted, and next she slid to the bottom like a diver. It was as though a living thing had disappeared beneath the waves.

—From Albert Kinross, "Torpedoed," *Atlantic Monthly*, December 1917.

CONSIDER THIS

1. How did Kinross and his shipmate react when the torpedo struck?
2. Using the description of his actions as clues, what do you think Kinross's job was on board the ship?

3. How did Kinross describe the last moments of the ship? What in his description tells you how he felt?

President Wilson's 1915 Position on War

The outbreak of war in Europe and submarine attacks on ships with Americans aboard led to heated debate in the United States. Some Americans wanted to remain neutral. They argued that the war did not involve America's interests. Others wanted the nation to join the war. In this speech on May 10, 1915, President Wilson expressed his feelings about America's role.

> The example of America must be a special example. The example of America must be the example not merely of peace because it will not fight, but of peace because peace is the healing and elevating influence of the world and strife is not … There is such a thing as a man being too proud to fight. There is such a thing as a nation being so right it does not need to convince others by force that it is right.
>
> —From Address of the President of the United States at Convention Hall, Philadelphia, Pennsylvania, May 10, 1915.

CONSIDER THIS

1. What example did Wilson believe the United States should set?
2. What tone do you think the president was trying to achieve in this speech? Do you think he was successful?

The Zimmermann Note

Arthur Zimmermann was Germany's foreign secretary. On January 19, 1917, he sent a telegram to the German ambassador in Mexico. In his note, Zimmermann proposed that Mexico and Germany unite in a war against the United States. British naval intelligence agents interrupted the message in transmission from Germany to Mexico. The British decoded it and sent the message to President Wilson. Wilson then had it released to the newspapers. The Zimmermann Note (or Zimmermann Telegram), as it came to be known, greatly strengthened the position of those Americans who supported going to war with Germany.

> Berlin, January 19, 1917
>
> On the first of February we intend to begin submarine warfare unrestricted. In spite of this, it is our intention to endeavor to keep neutral the United States of America.
>
> If this attempt is not successful, we propose an alliance on the following basis with Mexico: That we shall make war together and together make peace. We shall give general financial support, and it is understood that Mexico is to reconquer the lost territory in New Mexico, Texas, and Arizona. The details are left to you for settlement.
>
> You are instructed to inform the President of Mexico of the above in the greatest confidence as soon as it is certain that there will be an outbreak of war with the United States and suggest that the President of Mexico, on his own initiative, should communicate with Japan suggesting adherence at once to this plan;

at the same time, offer to mediate between Germany and Japan.

Please call to the attention of the President of Mexico that the employment of ruthless submarine warfare now promises to compel England to make peace in a few months.

—From Congressional Record, Vol. LVI, March 1, 1917, pt. I: pp. 680–681.

CONSIDER THIS

1. What did the German foreign secretary offer Mexico as a reward for its alliance with Germany against the United States?
2. How do you think Americans living in the Southwest reacted to the contents of the Zimmermann Note?

President Wilson's War Message to Congress

In 1916, President Wilson demanded that Germany stop unrestricted submarine warfare. The Germans agreed to the president's demand. They stated that they would not sink vessels without warning.

One year later, however, Germany said it would begin attacking passenger and freight ships without warning again. This action led to Wilson's call for war between Germany and the United States. The following are selections from Woodrow Wilson's War Message to Congress, delivered on April 2, 1917. Four days later, Congress passed the War Resolution, which brought the United States into the war.

KEY TERMS AND CONCEPTS

From the Zimmermann Note:

adherence The act of supporting a plan or maintaining one's loyalty.

compel To force.

initiative Desires and motivation.

ruthless Merciless or cruel.

From Woodrow Wilson's War Message:

autocracy A government in which one individual has all of the power.

belligerent A person or country involved in a war or conflict.

quarrel Argument or dispute.

solemn Serious or gloomy.

After his speech, Wilson commented to an aide, "My message of today was a message of death for our young men."

> Gentlemen of the Congress:
>
> I have called the Congress into extraordinary session because there are serious … choices of policy to be made …
>
> Vessels of every kind, whatever their flag, their character, their cargo, their destination, their errand, have been ruthlessly sent to the bottom without warning and without thought of help or mercy for

those on board, the vessels of friendly neutrals along with those of belligerents. Even hospital ships and ships carrying relief to the sorely bereaved and stricken people of Belgium … have been sunk with the same reckless lack of compassion or of principle …

I am not now thinking of the loss of property involved … Property can be paid for; the lives of peaceful and innocent people can not be. The present German submarine warfare against commerce is a warfare against mankind …

With a profound sense of the solemn and even tragical character of the step I am taking … I advise that the Congress declare the recent course of the Imperial German Government to be in fact nothing less than war against the Government and people of the United States …

We have no quarrel with the German people. We have no feeling towards them but one of sympathy and friendship …

One of the things that has served to convince us that the Prussian autocracy was not and could never be our friend is that from the very outset of the present war it has filled our unsuspecting communities and even our offices of government with spies and set criminal intrigues … against our national unity … Indeed it is now evident that its spies were here even before the war began …

We are glad, now that we see the facts … to fight thus for the ultimate peace of the world and for the

> liberation of its peoples, the German peoples included: for the rights of nations great and small and the privilege of men everywhere to choose their way of life ... The world must be made safe for democracy.
>
> —From Woodrow Wilson, War Message, 65th Congress, 1st Sess., Senate Doc. No. 5, Serial No. 7264 (Washington, DC, 1917).

CONSIDER THIS

1. What, in Wilson's opinion, forced the United States to declare war against Germany?
2. What was the ultimate goal of the United States in entering the war, according to Wilson?

The Debate Continues

The declaration of war did not end discussion about it. Some Americans were filled with dread at the thought of the huge sacrifices that lay ahead. Critics of the war included both government officials and citizens. They spoke out against US involvement. Some were pacifists, or individuals who opposed all war on moral grounds. Other critics viewed the conflict as being outside US interests. People who took a firm stand against the war often suffered for their beliefs. Some even went to jail for those beliefs.

Other Americans were anxious to end the war and saw their participation as the only way to bring it to a conclusion. They took patriotic pride in their willingness and ability to get the job done.

The government used propaganda, or information and imagery promoting a political agenda or point of view, to encourage people to support the war.

3 Differing Opinions

World War I saw the US federal government mobilize for war in new and interesting ways. Special commissions such as the Committee on Public Information were set up to build patriotic support. Writers wrote stirring songs and artists painted vivid posters to capture the public's attention. Pamphlets were printed in several languages explaining America's role in the war. School textbooks urged children to help out. Everyone was asked to pitch in and "do their bit." American factories and workers churned out goods as never before. That said, there were plenty of people who openly opposed the war.

An Opponent of the War Speaks Out

Not all Americans wanted the United States to join the fight. Pacifists spoke out against US involvement. Peace organizations sprang up throughout the nation.

Their members tried to influence congressional leaders and the newspapers.

In Congress, opponents of the war included Senator Robert M. La Follette of Wisconsin and Senator George W. Norris of Nebraska. Both spoke out against the war and were bitterly criticized for it. The following excerpt is from Senator Norris's speech before the Senate on April 4, 1917. It was two days before the War Resolution was passed.

> The resolution now before the Senate is a declaration of war. Before taking this momentous step, and while standing on the brink of this terrible vortex, we ought to pause and … consider the terrible consequences of the step we are about to take …
>
> The reason given by the President in asking Congress to declare war against Germany is that the German Government has declared certain war zones, within which, by the use of submarines, she sinks, without notice, American ships and destroys American lives …
>
> There are a great many American citizens who feel that we owe it as a duty to humanity to take part in the war. Many instances of cruelty and inhumanity can be found on both sides. Men are often biased in their judgment on account of their sympathy and their interests. To my mind, what we ought to have maintained from the beginning was the strictest neutrality. If we had done this, I do not believe we would have been on the verge of war at the present time.

> It is now demanded that the American citizens shall be used as insurance policies to guarantee the safe delivery of munitions of war to belligerent nations. The enormous profits of munition manufacturers, stockbrokers, and bond dealers must be still further increased by our entrance into the war. This has brought us to the present moment, when Congress … is about to declare war and engulf our country in the greatest holocaust that the world has ever known.
>
> —From Congressional Record, 65th Congress, 1st sess., Vol. LV, pt. I.

CONSIDER THIS

1. According to Senator Norris, who would benefit by America's entrance into the war?
2. What action did Norris urge his fellow senators to take?
3. Did Norris present a convincing argument? Why or why not?

A Citizen Explains His Opposition to the Draft

Once the United States was in the war, an army had to be assembled. On April 5, the government formally requested enforced service in the army. On June 5, 1917, ten million American men between the ages of twenty-one and thirty were required by the Selective Service Act to register their names with the government at local draft offices. In return, they received a green card with a number on it. Based on this card, they would be selected at random to fight.

The idea of a draft alarmed Americans. Many immigrants had fled enforced service in European armies when they came to America. They were especially upset by the new law. Opponents

KEY TERMS AND CONCEPTS

From George W. Norris's speech:

holocaust A destruction involving numerous deaths, such as a mass slaughter.

momentous Important.

munition Ammunition and other military supplies.

From Leonard Abbot's speech:

despotism Oppressive governmental power.

of conscription, or forced service, held protest meetings and asked that young men not register for the draft.

In the following excerpt from the *New York Herald*, Dr. Leonard Abbot, a speaker at an anti-conscription meeting in New York City, gives his reason for opposing the law.

> Conscription is immoral, unAmerican, and unconstitutional. Why in the name of humanity drag us into a war which we disapprove? ... Conscription is the thin entering wedge of military despotism ... Go to Europe and fight Germany if you want to, but do not try to drag us with you. ... The Government must have a guilty conscience when it arrests college boys and girls and tries to break up meetings that are opposed to its conscription.

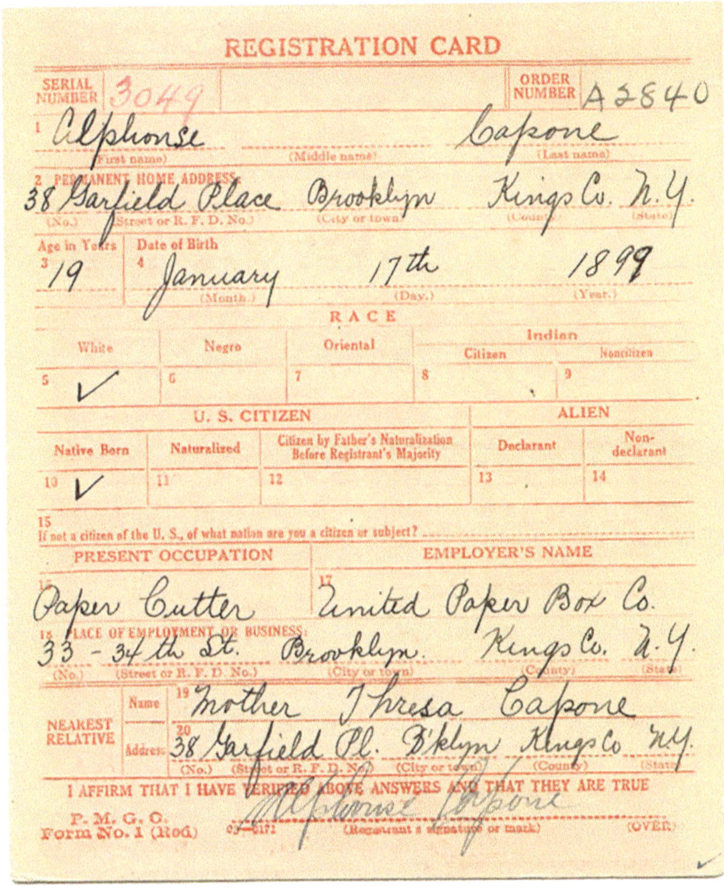

REGISTRATION CARD

SERIAL NUMBER 3049 | ORDER NUMBER A2840

1 Alphonse (First name) (Middle name) Capone (Last name)

2 PERMANENT HOME ADDRESS: 38 (No.) Garfield Place (Street or R. F. D. No.) Brooklyn (City or town) Kings Co. (County) N.Y. (State)

Age in Years 3 19 | Date of Birth 4 January (Month) 17th (Day) 1899 (Year)

RACE

White	Negro	Oriental	Indian Citizen	Indian Noncitizen
5 ✓	6	7	8	9

U. S. CITIZEN Native Born	Naturalized	Citizen by Father's Naturalization Before Registrant's Majority	ALIEN Declarant	Non-declarant
10 ✓	11	12	13	14

15 If not a citizen of the U. S., of what nation are you a citizen or subject?

PRESENT OCCUPATION 16 Paper Cutter | EMPLOYER'S NAME 17 United Paper Box Co.

18 PLACE OF EMPLOYMENT OR BUSINESS: 33 (No.) - 34th St. (Street or R. F. D. No.) Brooklyn (City or town) Kings Co. (County) N.Y. (State)

NEAREST RELATIVE Name 19 Mother Thresa Capone

Address 20 38 (No.) Garfield Pl. (Street or R. F. D. No.) B'klyn (City or town) Kings Co (County) N.Y. (State)

I AFFIRM THAT I HAVE VERIFIED ABOVE ANSWERS AND THAT THEY ARE TRUE

Alphonse Capone (Registrant's signature or mark)

P. M. G. O. Form No. 1 (Red) (OVER)

Although Alphonse "Al" Capone registered for selective service, as shown here, he would never serve in the US military. He did, however, go on to become an infamous Chicago gangster.

—From the *New York Herald*, June 5, 1917. Quoted in H. C. Peterson and Gilbert C. Fite, *Opponents of War, 1917–1918* (Madison, WI: University of Wisconsin Press, 1957).

CONSIDER THIS

1. On what grounds did the speaker oppose the draft?
2. What did the speaker fear the draft would lead to?
3. Think about writing a letter to the editor of the *New York Herald.* How would you present an argument for or against Dr. Abbot's statements?

Some Americans Demand Loyalty

Despite how vocal some people were about being against the war, their opinions weren't always welcome. Many Americans would not tolerate a difference of opinion. Dissenters were those who questioned US involvement or opposed war on religious grounds. The press condemned, or rejected, dissenters as disloyal. War protesters were often beaten by mobs. A common punishment was to force those suspected of disloyalty to kiss the American flag.

In the following excerpt from the *Sacramento Bee*, the writer expresses his opinion about what should happen to a teacher who questioned whether the United States was right to enter the war.

> It is time for her to be put out of the public schools and to be put out forever ... And when another [teacher] declares she doesn't believe the Board of Education has the right to interfere with her religion and her conscience ... then it is high time a drastic lesson be taught her ... to the effect that the religion of Liberty and the conscience of the United States are above her creed and her opinion, and that she will have to obey!

—From the *Sacramento Bee*, November 12, 1917. Quoted in H. C. Peterson and Gilbert C. Fite, *Opponents of War, 1917–1918* (Madison, WI: University of Wisconsin Press, 1957).

CONSIDER THIS

1. Which rights are discussed in this excerpt?
2. Why would the opinions of schoolteachers be important to a nation at war?

The Sedition Act

Once at war, the US government took drastic steps against those who might harm the nation's war effort. The Sedition Act (May 16, 1918) temporarily suspended freedom of the press and freedom of speech. Both freedoms are guaranteed in the Bill of Rights of the Constitution. The Sedition Act prevented people from speaking out against the war. It was an amendment, or addition, to the Espionage Act (June 15, 1917). The following is an excerpt from Section 3 of the Sedition Act.

> Whoever, when the United States is at war, shall willfully make or convey false reports or false statements with intent to interfere with the operation or success of the military or naval forces of the United States, or to promote the success of its enemies … or incite insubordination, disloyalty, mutiny, or refusal of duty … or shall willfully obstruct … the recruiting or enlistment service of the United States, or … shall willfully utter, print, write, or publish any disloyal, profane, scurrilous, or abusive language about the form of government of the United States … or shall willfully display the flag of any foreign enemy, or shall

Despite the threat of imprisonment, people protested the 1918 Sedition Act, which suspended Americans' rights to free speech and freedom of the press.

willfully ... urge, incite, or advocate any curtailment of production ... or advocate, teach, defend, or suggest the doing of any of the acts or things in this section enumerated and whoever shall by word or act support or favor the cause of any country with which the United States is at war ... shall be punished by a fine of not more than $10,000 or imprisonment for not more than twenty years, or both.

—From Statutes at Large, Volume XL (Washington, DC, 1918).

KEY TERMS AND CONCEPTS

From the Sedition Act:

curtailment The cutting off of something.

enlistment Enrollment in the armed forces.

incite To stir up.

insubordination Disobedience.

mutiny Resistance of authority.

scurrilous Vulgar or obscene.

CONSIDER THIS

1. Do you think the US government has the right to suspend the Constitution during wartime?
2. Do you think the punishments outlined fit the crimes?
3. Research the Alien and Sedition Acts of 1798. Compare and contrast them to the Sedition Act of 1918.

Americans Abroad

Whether or not people approved, Americans were sent to France in the summer of 1917. They came from many walks of life and parts of the nation. Thrown together in training camps, young men forged new friendships that would last throughout the war. While some reluctantly took up arms, others looked upon the war as the experience of a lifetime and a chance to see the world.

Despite the horrors of war, soldiers still had to carry on with their daily lives. For instance, these soldiers are walking the trenches delivering food.

4 The US Military Abroad

For most Americans, their arrival in France was their first encounter with another culture, another people, and another language. The war allowed them little time to appreciate these things, however. Young, inexperienced pilots got their first taste of air combat with the best of Germany's airmen. Their deadly duels were fought above the chaos of the battlefields below. For the ordinary foot soldier, the war was far from glamorous. Those who survived would never forget the mud of the trenches, the terror of being bombarded day and night, the boredom of a soldier's routine, or the horror of combat. Men killed in the fighting never returned home. They were buried where they fell, with their brothers-in-arms in the fields of France.

Diverse Soldiers

Draftees into the US Army came from all parts of the nation and from many different backgrounds. They were southerners and midwesterners, city boys and farm boys. Some young men had college educations, while others could barely read and write. Regardless of where they came from and what they did before the war, the young men were about to become soldiers. Camps were set up around the country with the purpose of turning civilians into soldiers.

African Americans in particular saw the war as a means to advance their long struggle for equality—even if it meant dying in battle. "If this is our country, then this is our war," announced W. E. B. Du Bois. He was a prominent African American intellectual. Du Bois wrote that "unstinting patriotism would lead to the right to vote and the right to work and the right to live without insult." Yet not all Americans favored allowing black people in the armed services.

Immigration and the Armed Forces

Hundreds of thousands of southern and eastern Europeans came to America in the years just before World War I. When the United States joined the war in 1917, these newcomers found themselves drafted into the army of their adopted nation. The foreign-born draftees quickly had to learn new ways, and the army had to find ways to teach them to be soldiers.

The following account is by Fred Rindge. He was the secretary of the International Committee of the YMCA (Young Men's Christian Association).

> I went to the great cantonments expecting to see a great body of Americans. I found thousands of

Italians, Poles, Russians, Rumanians, Greeks, and others—all potential Americans, to be sure, but with a long way to travel yet! In each of the several camps of 30,000 to 40,000 men I found 4,000 to 5,000 who understand little English and speak still less …

I talked with scores of colonels and other officers, and all agreed that this was one of their greatest problems. One regiment had about eighty percent "foreigners." Many had fifty percent. Whole companies were made up mostly of Poles or some other foreign nationality. Imagine these fellows from the slums of Chicago, Milwaukee, Detroit, Cleveland, New York, getting off their trains, being taken to camp … given instructions which they could little understand, and beginning … a life as new and strange to them as aeroplaning would be for you and me! …

To build real soldiers out of this material is a slow process, requiring infinite patience. One captain told me this as a joke on himself.

"Today when drilling my men I was provoked so many times by one fellow who refused to listen or obey orders that I sailed into him before the whole company. After I had completed what I thought was a rather impressive speech one of the non-commissioned officers saluted and said, 'Excuse me, Captain, but that man doesn't understand a word you're saying!'"

—From Fred G. Rindge Jr., "Uncle Sam's Adopted Nephews," *Harper's Magazine,* July 1918.

KEY TERMS AND CONCEPTS

From Fred Rindge's account:

cantonment Temporary living quarters for soldiers.

sail into To attack sharply.

From Elmer Sherwood's journal:

barrage Rapid fire.

Boche Germans.

demoralize To weaken the spirit of.

feeble Weak.

howitzers Short cannons.

intonation Sound.

75s French 75mm guns.

stupendous Tremendous.

CONSIDER THIS

1. What was the army's main problem concerning the foreign-born recruits?
2. Why might a newcomer be opposed to fighting in the war? Why might he want to take part?

The Battle of Saint-Mihiel

By the time Americans entered the war, it had become a mind- and body-numbing round of raids and assaults on the enemy trenches. These assaults always followed the same pattern regardless of which side launched the attack. Before the light of day, the attackers' heavy guns would start firing nonstop. Their fire was aimed at the guns and the trenches of the opposing army. The goal: to soften up the enemy. Then, at the sound of a whistle or a shout, the attacking soldiers would climb out of their trenches. They would hurdle across the lip of earth that protected them, and run, crawl, or zigzag through an area covered with barbed wire, holes made by explosive shells, and blasted tree stumps.

During this mad dash through no-man's-land, the enemy would fire with all its might. Few soldiers actually survived these assault waves. Most were cut down by machine-gun fire or exploding shells. If a trench was actually taken by the attacking soldiers, it was almost a sure bet that the enemy would get it back during the counterassault. This is the way the war was fought.

Corporal Elmer Sherwood was twenty years old in 1918. He was a soldier in the Forty-Second Division. It was unofficially called the Rainbow Division. Sherwood served as a scout, or someone in search of information, and telephone-line repairman. He took part in the Battle of Saint-Mihiel. It was one of the most famous World War I battles involving the American forces. Over four days in September 1918, the Americans captured territory that the Germans had held for four years. The victory was a great boost for America's spirit. It proved to the Allies that US soldiers could plan and carry out a big military undertaking.

Corporal Sherwood kept a diary during his time in the army. Here are his comments about his experiences in battle.

September 12—The zero hour was 1:05 a.m., the heavy artillery starting it off. The earth seemed to give way when the rest of our guns joined in the stupendous and fierce barrage ... We could scarcely distinguish the deep intonation of our own howitzers from the reports of the 75s.

For four hours ... our messengers of death were hurled into enemy territory. Then at 5:00 our infantry preceded by tanks went over the top ...

The boys of our division leaped ahead of the clumsy tanks and pressed forward in irresistible waves to the German trenches.

The enemy artillery reply was feeble, though the infantry machine-gun and rifle fire was more menacing.

Our artillery fire in the first place demoralized enemy resistance, and the Boche are surrendering in droves. Surely they must regret giving up these luxurious dugouts and trenches which they have lived in for four years.

—From Elmer W. Sherwood, *Diary of a Rainbow Veteran, Written at the Front* (Terre Haute, IN: Moore-Langen Company, 1929).

CONSIDER THIS

1. How did the battle begin, according to Sherwood's account?
2. Why do you think it began this way?

The Harlem Hellfighters

African Americans have always served in America's fighting forces. From the Revolutionary War to the Spanish-American War, black soldiers took up arms in the nation's defense even when the nation didn't consider them citizens.

When the United States joined World War I, black Americans were among those drafted into the armed services. The army was strictly segregated in 1917, however. This meant that black draftees served in regiments consisting of only black men. One of the most famous of these units was the 15th New York. It eventually became the 369th Infantry Regiment of the 93rd Division. The 15th grew to 1,378 men and about 50 officers.

Even though the Hellfighters were famous for their victories in World War I, they still faced discrimination when they returned to the United States.

Once in France, the men of the 369th Infantry spent nearly two hundred days on the front lines. The German soldiers called the men of the 369th the "Hellfighters" because of their bravery in battle. The name stuck. The infantry became known as the "Harlem Hellfighters" in tribute to Harlem, a famous black neighborhood in New York City and the home of the 15th New York.

The following excerpt is from Haywood Butt's remembrance of his days in the 369th. Butt was born in North Carolina in 1897 and moved to Harlem in 1912.

> Our unit started in 1913. There wasn't much to it at first. Boys used to drill with broomsticks up on 63rd Street, at St. Cyprian's Church. We drilled once a week ... We didn't get any heavy combat training until we shipped out of the city up to Peekskill and Camp Whitman upstate ... In August 1917, when we shipped out of the city ... Pershing wanted us to become laborers and to take our arms from us. That would have been sort of a disgrace, to disarm us. We went over to a New York regiment, and they didn't want us. None of the white units did, so we went around to the French. We fought side by side with the French ... We fought in the Champagne. I was on the front lines for 191 straight days ...
>
> —From Jess Kisseloff, *You Must Remember This: An Oral History of Manhattan from the 1890s to World War II* (New York: Schocken Books, 1989).

KEY TERMS AND CONCEPTS

From Haywood Butt's account:

Champagne A region of France.

Pershing John J. Pershing, the leader of American forces in Europe.

St. Cyprian's Church A church in New York City attended primarily by black immigrants from the Caribbean.

From Emmett Scott's account:

retire To retreat or withdraw from danger.

CONSIDER THIS

1. How did Haywood Butt and the other men train at first? Why do you think they had to train this way?
2. Why do you think the white units refused to join up with the 369th but French units took no issue?

A Refusal to Give up

The 369th became famous for the bravery of its men and the dedication of its commanding officer, Colonel William Hayward. It fought in some of the bloodiest battles of the war—the Argonne

Forest, Château-Thierry, and Belleau Wood. The 369th served as part of the 161st French Division. Because of its contribution to France, the entire regiment was awarded the French Croix de Guerre. This is France's highest military honor. They were not given any similar honor by the US government at the time.

All Harlem Hellfighters, like Private Ed Williams, pictured here, received the French Croix de Guerre in 1918. Only Henry Johnson received a US equivalent: the Medal of Honor. It was awarded by President Barack Obama in 2015, eighty-six years after Johnson's death.

This excerpt is from Emmett J. Scott's *Official History of the American Negro in the World War.* Scott was special assistant for Negro affairs to the US secretary of war. This selection illustrates how the regiment gained its fame.

The regiment came up to the German front lines ... Some one suggested that they turn back ... "We are going through there or we don't come back," was what Colonel Hayward said as he ... grabbed a gun from a soldier, and darted out ahead ... A French General ordered the regiment to retire, but Colonel Hayward ... cried: "My men never retire. They go forward, or they die!"

—From Emmett J. Scott, *Scott's Official History of the American Negro in the World War* (New York: Arno Press and the New York Times, 1969).

CONSIDER THIS

1. How did the American commander of the 369th react to the counterattack?
2. Why do you think he disobeyed the French general's order?
3. What thoughts and feelings may have motivated Colonel Hayward?

A Modern War

Although some eagerly traveled abroad and others fought with bravery, World War I was terrifying for many because it was so different from prior warfare. It was the first modern war. World War I was fought not just on land and at sea, but in the air as well. Deadly new weapons were developed and used by both sides.

Large-scale chemical warfare started in World War I. The Central and Allied powers used chlorine, phosgene, and mustard gas to attack their enemies. Chemical weapons were just one of the things that made the war so deadly.

5

New Technologies

One of the things that made World War I so devastating was the new weapon-related technology. Soldiers were subjected to fire from massive guns mounted on railroad tracks, had bombs dropped on them from the air, and were suffocated by poisonous gases released over the ground. Tanks, armored vehicles of all kinds, airplanes, balloons, and submarines were just a few of the weapons of destruction that were used during the war.

In the Face of Change

Despite these technical innovations, military leaders still followed old-fashioned battle tactics. These tactics included stand-up assaults in which wave after wave of troops would march across a piece of land. This was done in an often pointless attempt to seize the enemy's position. These assaults were mass slaughters.

Many soldiers in World War I were killed by shrapnel from shells exploding around them. Shrapnel are fragments from bombs or shells. What shrapnel did not accomplish was carried out by bullets fired from rifles and machine guns. The amount of ammunition fired during World War I was so great that today's visitors to the battlefields still uncover shell casings.

A Gas Attack

The war also saw the introduction of chemical warfare. On April 22, 1915, German troops released gas containing chlorine over the Allied lines on the Western Front. The Allied troops were caught by complete surprise. The following newspaper accounts from the *New York Tribune* describe the gas attack and its effect.

> North of France, April 24.— … The nature of the gasses … remain[s] a mystery. Whatever gas it is, it spreads rapidly and remains close to the ground. It is believed not to be specially deadly—one that rather overpowers its victims and puts them hors de combat without killing many.
>
> Boulogne, April 25.—The gaseous vapor which the Germans used against the French divisions near Ypres last Thursday … introduces a new element into warfare. The attack … was preceded by the rising of a cloud of vapor, greenish gray and iridescent. That vapor settled to the ground like a swamp mist and drifted toward the French trenches on a brisk wind. Its effect on the French was a violent nausea and faintness, followed by an utter collapse …
>
> The work of sending out the vapor was done from the advanced German trenches. Men garbed in dress

resembling the harness of a [deep-sea] diver and armed with ... generators about three feet high and connected with ordinary hose pipe turned the vapor loose towards the French lines ...

In addition to this, the Germans appear to have fired ordinary explosive shells loaded with some chemical which ... produced violent watering of the eyes, so that the men overcome ... were practically blinded for some hours.

The effect of the noxious trench gas seems to be slow in wearing away. The men come out of their nausea in a state of utter collapse. Some of the rescued have already died from the aftereffects.

—From the *New York Tribune*, April 25 and 27, 1915.

CONSIDER THIS

1. How do you think the Allies reacted to Germany's use of poison gas?
2. Why do you think that Germans chose to use gas as opposed to gunfire?

An Aerial Gunner's First Flight

The development of the airplane also changed warfare. World War I was the first major conflict in which the airplane was used as a weapon. When America joined the fight in 1917, it had around fifty outdated planes. America's Air Service was small compared with those of Great Britain, France, and Germany. Despite its unpreparedness and lack of well-trained pilots, the Army Air

KEY TERMS AND CONCEPTS

From the *New York Tribune*:

hors de combat Unable to fight or act because of injury.

noxious Poisonous or harmful.

Ypres A town in northwestern Belgium that was the site of three different battles during World War I.

Service proved its worth. By the end of the war, its pilots had brought down over seven hundred enemy airplanes.

Before the United States entered the war, however, many adventurous Americans had already joined the conflict in Europe. They had gone to England and France in 1914 and enlisted in the army and air services of those countries. Arch Whitehouse was one of them. He was born in England in 1895 and moved to the United States in 1905. His family settled in Livingston, New Jersey. When World War I broke out, Whitehouse enlisted in the British armed services and was put to work grooming horses. This was not much fun for a young man seeking the thrill of combat.

Before long, Whitehouse discovered the Royal Flying Corps and transferred to a unit of battle planes. He learned to be an aerial gunner, or someone who fires guns from a plane. Eventually, he became a pilot. In later years, Whitehouse became an author of numerous books on World War I. The following description is from his autobiography, *The Fledgling*. It describes his introduction to being an aerial gunner.

"Get up and take a look around," [Captain Clement] yelled over the whine of the flying wires … "Then fire at the target." …

Clement curled the plane over in a tight turn, and I closed my eyes until I sensed that we had straightened out. When my intestines agreed to stay where they belonged, I knew we were flying reasonably level—and manfully took over my gun.

Down we went … I did press the trigger, and I did aim the gun; but how I put such a beautiful burst of forty-seven rounds into one of those panels was something only the gods decided.

We circled once more. Clement shut off the engine, and to my grim relief we landed safely beside the target.

"Holy smoke!" Captain Clement gasped. "… Keep this up, young fellow, and you can fly with me any day."

—From Arch Whitehouse, *The Fledgling: An Autobiography* (New York: Duell, Sloan and Pearce, 1964).

CONSIDER THIS

1. Why do you think that Captain Clement had Whitehouse firing at the targets during his first time in the air?
2. Why do you think that Whitehouse joined the British armed services?

Some American aviators, like Edward F. Hinkle, served in the Lafayette Escadrille, a unit in the French army that transferred to the US military after the United States joined the war in 1917.

Danger in the Air

The use of airplanes by the Allies and Germany made World War I different from other wars. Dogfights—air battles between enemies—were fought over the Western Front. These fights were often within view of the soldiers on the ground. During these battles, a pilot would try to disable the enemy airplane by firing at it with his guns. The goal was to force the enemy pilot to crash his airplane or withdraw from the fight. Sometimes a pilot would let his enemy live if he showed fairness or unusual skill and daring in combat.

The war in the air sparked the American imagination. Aviators who succeeded in shooting down at least five enemy planes were called "aces." They became heroes of the press. Their deeds of daring became legendary.

A pilot's life was not all aerial warfare, however. Pilots also flew observation missions over enemy lines. The purpose of these missions was to observe the movements of the enemy. During these flights, the pilot was accompanied by an observer-cameraman whose job was to take pictures of the battlefield below. Photography was thus united with aviation in the carrying out of war. In the following excerpt, Lieutenant Samuel P. Mandell recalls a memorable flight with his observer.

> Old Fiske was standing up on the seat in back shooting ... At the same time I dove to get a shot ... with my gun. I heard a sort of a crash ... I could hardly believe my eyes, but Fiske had fallen out of his cockpit when his gun broke loose from its fastenings ... As I watched him over my shoulder, he gradually wound his way up the fuselage. He got a-straddle of it and gradually slid up ... and dove head first into his seat ...

KEY TERMS AND CONCEPTS

From Samuel P. Mandell's account:
fuselage The main body of an aircraft.
Old Fiske Lieutenant Gardiner H. Fiske, who was flying as an observer in a training maneuver.

From the *Atlantic Monthly*:
cab The interior of the tank with the operational controls.
devise To create.
gaily Easily.
raucously Noisily.
sullen Gloomy.

—From Frank Freidel, *Over There: The Story of America's First Great Overseas Crusade* (Boston: Little, Brown and Company, 1964).

CONSIDER THIS

1. Which would you have preferred, to be a soldier in the trenches or a pilot in the sky? Why?

Tanks

Tanks were among the new weapons that appeared in World War I. They were first used by the British Royal Tank Corps and later by the Americans. Tanks were plated with metal and fitted

Tanks were used for warfare for the first time in World War I. They were introduced during the Battle of the Somme in September 1916.

with belts in place of wheels. They could go where animals and men could not. They could run down the enemy, travel over ground with shell holes, and plow through barbed wire.

Tanks had their drawbacks, though. They were clumsy. They often broke down. Additionally, they could be blown up by antitank mines. For these reasons, in World War I, tanks never replaced machine guns, cannon, or rifles.

The following is a description, which appeared in an article in the *Atlantic Monthly* magazine in 1917, of several kinds of tanks.

The Mark IV Tank is a slow and sullen dinosaur. Four miles an hour is his limit. Frequently … he mounts a platform on his back and carries a sixty-pounder gun; or hauls a sledge, like an ox team, to pull big howitzers over shell craters. The Mark V is the next step upward in evolution. He is good for five miles an hour, has made nine, and one man can drive him. When I climbed down into the hot and whirring middle of a Mark V, heard the gears squeal and roar, and saw through the eye-slits the ground swinging under us, I knew how a steam roller might feel … Nothing could stop our many ton, hundred and fifty horse power. We came to a trench, swung up, so easily, and down with scarcely a quiver, and so on about our business.

The Whippet … is light … and carried a cab like a camel's hump. The Whippet has two engines. As she runs her eight, ten … twenty miles an hour, she squeals raucously. At a rock or stump … she whirls with unbelievable rapidity till your eyes are looking one way and your stomach another. She rumbles gaily over the field, sees a trench, rises on her hind quarters, drops below sky-line with a teeth-shaking bump, grips the further bank, rolls up screaming, and charges off for more. Never was devised a more dangerous … engine of warfare than this.

—From Henry Seidel Canby, "Education by Violence," *Atlantic Monthly,* 1917.

CONSIDER THIS

1. How does the writer use animal imagery to describe the tanks?
2. Do the tanks described in this excerpt sound terrifying or old-fashioned?
3. Do you think the writer approves or disapproves of tanks as weapons of war? How can you tell?

In the Face of Danger

Despite the new dangers presented by World War I, soldiers carried on. Even more surprising, however, were civilians who volunteered their time and sometimes sacrificed their lives in support of the war. In addition to men who volunteered, some women joined the armed forces for the first time.

Civilians volunteered to do a variety of work. Although these jobs didn't always involve fighting, they sometimes put these individuals in harm's way. For instance, ambulance drivers drove through battlefields to collect the sick and wounded.

6 Male and Female Volunteers

People from all walks of life joined the war effort. Young men from the United States traveled overseas to volunteer as ambulance drivers. They took on the dangerous job of shuttling wounded soldiers back from the front. Young women went overseas to help out in any way they could. Some took jobs settling refugees displaced from their homes. Doctors and nurses from American hospitals volunteered to tend the wounded. Many more used their talents to raise money for the Allies. There was no end of war work for those who wanted to help.

Young American Ambulance Drivers

John Masefield was an English poet and writer. He was born in 1878 and went to sea while still a boy. He traveled the world, often doing odd jobs and writing poetry. His best-known poems are about the sea and seafaring men.

However, Masefield also wrote newspaper and magazine articles, military and naval histories, and children's books. During World War I, he went to France, where he observed the war at close range.

Even before the United States joined the war, many Americans had decided to help France. Some helped people who had been driven from their homes by the war. Others volunteered to help transport wounded soldiers to hospitals. At first, the volunteer ambulance drivers provided their own cars. As the war dragged on, the ambulance of choice became the Ford Model T. Driving it was a challenge. The Model T was fitted with three foot pedals and a hand lever. In addition to operating the vehicle, the driver had to be able to repair it.

In the following excerpt from a magazine article, Masefield writes about the work of the American volunteer ambulance drivers.

> After supper, in the last of the light, the ambulance-cars are made ready; the two drivers in each car put on their steel helmets and take their gas masks, and the convoy moves out, car by car, toward the Postes de Secours, where they will find the wounded. Some camps are so far from the front that the first part of the journey up can be done with headlights. All roads leading to the front are crowded with men or wagons going up or coming down. The image of this war will be of a convoy of many wagons, driven by tired men, going on and on along the darkness of a road ... each man seeing no more of the war than the tail-board of the wagon in front.
>
> As the car runs in the open, the drivers see the star-shells going up and up, and bursting into white stars, and pausing and drifting slowly down ... They are the most beautiful things in modern war and almost the most terrible. In this open space the drivers can

see for some miles over the battlefield. As far as the eye can see, the lights are rising and falling. There is not much noise, but a sort of mutter of battle with explosions now and then. Perhaps ten miles away, there is fighting, for in that quarter the sky glimmers as though with summer lightning; the winks and flashes of the guns shake and die across the heaven.

Just overhead as the car passes comes a blasting, shattering crash which is like sudden death. Then another and another follow ... right overhead. On the tail of each crash comes the crying of the shell, passing overhead like a screech-owl, till it is far away in the enemy lines, where it bursts. Above the engines one shell's noise is heard; the screech of its rush comes very near, there is a flash ahead, a burst, and the patter of falling fragments. Another shell bursts behind the car, and another on the road in front; the car goes around the new shell-hole and passes on.

This is "the front."

[The ambulance drivers arrive at the Poste de Secours.]

The drivers go down the sloping path into the cellars. Presently the sick arrive, haggard and white, but able to walk and the ambulances are free to go. The stretchers are passed into the ambulances, the sick are helped on to seats, they are covered with blankets, and the doors are closed. Shells from the enemy rush overhead and burst in a village which lies on the road home. They are strafing the village;

the cars have a fair chance of being blown to pieces. The drivers start their engines and turn the cars for home; the rain drives in their faces as they go, and along the road in front of them the shells flash at intervals, lighting the tree-stumps.

These drivers are the very pick and flower of American life. The greater number of them young men on the threshold of life. All life lies before them in their own country, but they have … come to help France in her hour of need. All live a life of danger and risk death nightly.

—From John Masefield, "The Harvest of the Night," *Harper's Magazine*, May 1917.

CONSIDER THIS

1. How does the writer use words to paint a picture of the front?
2. Why do you think this piece is called "The Harvest of the Night"?

A Doctor at the Front

Hundreds of thousands of soldiers were killed outright in battle during World War I. Many more died of injuries or disease. Shrapnel from exploding shells killed or disfigured countless soldiers. Poison gas burned soldiers' lungs and eyes. Foot infections led to the loss of toes and feet. Hours spent in muddy trenches resulted in deadly fevers. Army doctors saw wounds they had never seen before.

Dr. Harvey Cushing was a surgeon in World War I. Early in the war, he served with a Harvard Unit in the American Ambulance

KEY TERMS AND CONCEPTS

From John Masefield's article:

convoy A group of vehicles organized for protection.

haggard Rough in appearance.

Postes de Secours Rescue stations.

strafe To sweep over with gunfire.

tail-board A tailgate.

From Harvey Cushing's journal:

morass A swamp, or a state of confusion.

Hospital in Paris. From there, he went to Flanders, a region of western Belgium. There he worked with Britain's Royal Army Medical Corps.

When the United States joined the war, Dr. Cushing was appointed a senior consultant to the Medical Headquarters of the American Expeditionary Force. He saw firsthand the suffering of French, British, and American soldiers. During his time at the front—1915 to 1918—Dr. Cushing kept a journal of his experiences. His observations from the 1917 Battle of Ypres are included here.

Operating under fire—

Tuesday, July 31—What may go down in history as the third battle of Ypres … opened to day …

Harvey Cushing was a leading neurosurgeon, someone who operates on the brain, in the early twentieth century. His methods are still important for brain surgery.

> August 1, 1:30 a.m.—Pitch black, pouring rain, and has been … nearly all this fearful day … The preoperative hut is still packed with untouched cases, so caked with mud that it's a task even to strip them and find out what they've got.
>
> August 2, 2:30 a.m.— … The preoperation room is still crowded …The news, too, is very bad. The greatest battle of history is floundering in a morass …
>
> 10:30 p.m.—Operating again all day, and finished up an hour ago. A lot of wounded must have drowned in the mud. One of today's cases was a young Scot … He had lain … in the protection of a shell hole … —the water up to his waist—for twelve hours …
>
> —From Harvey Cushing, *From a Surgeon's Journal: 1915–1918* (Boston: Little, Brown, and Company, 1936).

CONSIDER THIS

1. Why do you think a doctor would keep a journal of the war?
2. What additional difficulties do you think operating in the battlefield presented?

Women in the Signal Corps

In the nineteenth century, American women weren't generally allowed to serve in the armed forces, though some brave women disguised themselves as men and joined war efforts dating back to the American Revolution. World War I, however, saw the first large-scale enlistment of women into the military. In 1917, the

US Navy announced that it would enlist women. Approximately eleven thousand women served in the US Naval Reserves from 1917 to the end of the war in 1918. The yeomanettes, as the women were called, worked as clerks, draftswomen, translators, camouflage designers, and recruiters. These were all jobs once held by men.

America's need for women workers extended into other areas as well. In 1917, the War Department called for telephone operators to serve in France. They had to be able to speak both English and French. They would be acting as interpreters between the French and American commanders. The women were carefully chosen for their skill and character. They would have knowledge of troop movements, so their trustworthiness was of the utmost importance. More than seven thousand women applied to be members of the Signal Corps. About two hundred of these were selected and sent to Europe. The first unit of telephone operators was led by Grace Banker. She was a former instructor of the American Telephone and Telegraph Company.

Once in Europe, the women of the Signal Corps were nicknamed "Hello Girls." They served at US Army headquarters in France and in towns in England and France. During the last months of the war, the women operated communications equipment behind the front lines. The following is a recollection of a Signal Corps operator. She tells what it was like to bridge the gap between American and French ways of communication during World War I.

> When you wished to call over the French line, you said, "J'ecoute." ("I listen.") ... The conversation [with the French phone operator] would begin with ... pleasantries ... All this had to be in honeyed tones ... And mademoiselle would reply, "Ah, oui," in a languid sort of way ... If you asked for one place too often, you committed a serious blunder, for the result would be something like this: "You are unbearable, you ring

In addition to working the switchboards, some women of the Signal Corps were also responsible for ground and aerial photography.

too much. Je coupe! (I disconnect)" and—bing, the line would be lost and that was an end to that ...

—From Lettie Gavin, *American Women in World War I: They Also Served* (Niwot: University Press of Colorado, 1997).

CONSIDER THIS

1. The writer describes the way she dealt with the French operator. What did she have to do to get the operator's attention?
2. Why was the work of the telephone operators so important during the war?

KEY TERMS AND CONCEPTS

From the Signal Corps operator's recollection:
blunder A mistake.
languid Slow.
pleasantries Polite social remarks.

From Eva Belle Babcock's account:
sedative A drug intended to calm someone down.

A Nurse Recounts Shell Shock

The need for doctors and nurses during World War I was also great. Many American health care workers answered the call. Volunteer nurses were attached to the Army Nurse Corps. It was headed by Julia Catherine Stimson. Near the front, nurses set up mobile tent hospitals to receive the wounded. They cleaned the wounded, took part in operations, and gave comfort to the dying.

Sometimes the women worked forty or fifty hours without rest. Once their work was done, the nurses took the tent hospital down and moved to the next area of need. Eva Belle Babcock was one of the nurses sent to France in 1917. In the following account, she comments on her state after the war ended.

> I couldn't sleep. They found me walking in the street wearing just my pajamas, saying I had to get back on duty ... That's when I wound up in the hospital

> myself. They gave me warm baths and some sedatives. About then, my father hadn't heard from me in a long time, so he wrote to Washington. They wrote back that I was ... suffering from "shell shock."
>
> —From Lettie Gavin, *American Women in World War I: They Also Served* (Niwot: University Press of Colorado, 1997).

CONSIDER THIS

1. Why did the writer have a difficult time getting over her experience?
2. Why do you think warm baths and sedatives were used as treatments?

The Home Front

While those Americans who found themselves engaged in the war suffered both immediate and lasting effects, the war was also felt back in the United States. Americans geared up to fight the war with everything they had. Everyone—from men to women to children—was called to action. People were encouraged to donate to the war effort. Factories were encouraged to produce more. Everyone was encouraged to play his or her part in securing victory.

World War I propaganda often encouraged Americans to buy bonds to help fund the war.

7 *The War Effort*

The war effort had a far reach. The Food Administration urged housewives to substitute other foods for meat and wheat on specific days of the week. The National War Garden Commission asked families to plant gardens and to can fruits and vegetables from these gardens. "Can Vegetables, Fruit, and the Kaiser, too" proclaimed a poster for the commission. The Treasury Department staged huge rallies during which all Americans were asked to buy Liberty bonds to fund the war. The War Industries Board persuaded factories to increase their production of war goods. However, the war had a far greater reach than one generated by government offices.

Women and Children

The war effort even involved children. They were told to save quarters and use them to buy war savings stamps. Children were also encouraged to save ordinary household goods such as old glass and empty cans for reuse by war factories. Schools taught lessons around the themes of patriotism, service, and self-sacrifice. "Every patriotic American can serve by being loyal—by working, saving, giving," proclaimed *Our Country's Call to Service: A Manual of Patriotic Activities Through the Schools*, published in 1918.

During this time, a new kind of worker appeared in the US workplace. American women who did not join the war abroad welcomed the chance to enter the workforce. They willingly took over as mechanics, welders, machinists, postal workers, and elevator operators. These were jobs once held only by men. These women worked long hours to help the war effort while also managing to work at home.

The Great Migration

The war also witnessed the mass movement of people from one part of the nation to another. There were shortages of workers in the factories of the North and Midwest. These shortages created opportunities for hundreds of thousands of African Americans from the South. During the war years, black people left the heavily agricultural South and traveled north. They established black neighborhoods in cities such as Chicago, Detroit, and New York. The war was changing America in important ways.

A Different Type of Call to Action

The United States was committed to victory. However, the cost of supporting an army overseas was huge. The government asked the American people to help finance the war effort and held four campaigns to sell Liberty bonds. Everyone was asked to buy bonds, from regular citizens to movie stars. In the end, the United States made more than $20 billion for the war. That would be equivalent to over $366 billion in 2019.

Approximately six million African Americans migrated from the South to the North in search of better opportunities between 1916 and 1970.

Emmett Scott, the special assistant secretary of war, launched the Fourth Liberty Loan Campaign among African Americans in the District of Columbia in October 1918. Here is part of his speech.

> It is not a white man's war. It is not a black man's war. It is a war of all the people under the Stars and Stripes …
>
> Already, the Negro has responded promptly and cheerfully to the call for his man-power …
>
> Now comes a fourth call for financial aid …
>
> The success of the Fourth Liberty Loan subscriptions … should be the absorbing mission of colored ministers,

editors, teachers, merchants, lawyers, doctors, and speakers and workers ...

—From Emmett J. Scott, *Scott's Official History of the American Negro in the World War* (New York: Arno Press and the New York Times, 1969).

CONSIDER THIS

1. In light of the prejudice African Americans had long endured, how do you think black people responded to this speech?

On the Lookout

In addition to raising money, the government wanted to make sure everyone was in support of the war. The Committee on Public Information was set up in 1917. It was responsible for stirring up patriotism and support. Its director was newspaperman George Creel. The committee hired men and women to deliver brief but stirring patriotic speeches. These were on themes such as "Save Food," "Buy Bonds," and "Give Until It Hurts." These speeches were delivered in places such as movie theaters and concert halls. Boy Scouts were given the job of handing out patriotic pamphlets. Famous artists and writers were hired to draw patriotic posters and write advertisements in support of the war. These speeches weren't only for encouragement. Citizens were also warned to be on the lookout for spies. Here is an excerpt from the committee's warning.

German agents are everywhere, eager to gather scraps of news about our men, our ships, our munitions. It is still possible to get such information through to Germany, where thousands of these fragments ... are pieced together into a whole which spells death to American soldiers and danger to American homes.

- Do not discuss in public, or with strangers, any news of troop and transport movements, or bits of gossip as to our military preparations, which come into your possession.

- Do not permit your friends in service to tell you—or write you—"inside" facts about where they are, what they are doing and seeing.

- Do not become a tool of the Hun by passing on the malicious, disheartening rumors which he so eagerly sows.

- And do not wait until you catch someone putting a bomb under a factory. Report the man who spreads pessimistic stories, divulges—or seeks—confidential military information, cries for peace, or belittles our efforts to win the war.

Send the names of such persons, even if they are in uniform, to the Department of Justice, Washington. Give all the details you can, with names of witnesses if possible …

Committee on Public Information
8 Jackson Place
Washington, D.C.

—From Committee on Public Information poster, date unknown.

KEY TERMS AND CONCEPTS

From the Committee on Public Information's warning:

belittle To make something seem unimportant or small.
disheartening Causing to lose hope or enthusiasm.
divulge To make known or public.
Hun An outdated, now offensive term used to describe Germans.
malicious Showing the desire to harm someone.
pessimistic Characterized by negativity or gloominess.

CONSIDER THIS

1. According to this warning, what were some of the dangers facing the United States during the war?
2. How do you think this warning affected German Americans?
3. How did this warning treat Americans' constitutional liberties?

Women at Work

World War I was the first time in US history that women in large numbers took jobs traditionally held by men. They became conductors on streetcars, automobile mechanics, and shipyard workers. Many worked on the assembly lines of factories making tanks, trucks, and munitions. For the most part, women liked the challenge of their new lives. The attitude of these women is described in the following excerpt from an interview by Norma Kastl, an interviewer in a service bureau for women workers. Her interview appeared in a magazine published during the war.

> The Government gas mask factory has proved a most interesting field for many artists, musicians, and stage women. One well-known portrait painter is now spending her days in turning over little brass disks and carefully inspecting both sides. Another woman who has created several famous character parts on Broadway gets up every morning at half past five and takes the early train into New York to get to the factory at eight o'clock. During the recent speeding-up period, caused by urgent calls from our armies overseas, she reached home often as late as ten or eleven at night. But did she mind? Not she! "I would not have missed it for anything," she said. "It has been one of the richest experiences of my life—meeting all the wonderful women who are there ... and all the time feeling that I was being really useful to the boys on the other side."
>
> —From Norma B. Kastl, "Wartime, the Place and the Girl," *Independent* magazine, 1918.

CONSIDER THIS

1. Why do you think women were so happy to be a part of the war effort? Do you think it was the war itself or the opportunity to do new types of work?
2. Why do you think artists, musicians, and stage women were the people who found the gas mask factory the most interesting?

Although women had worked in factories like textile mills since the mid-nineteenth century, the war provided an influx of new and different opportunities for women.

War Reporting

While some creatives joined the war effort like the women described above, other artists continued to work on their crafts. The reason we know so much about the war today is that countless journalists, poets, and writers took to the page to describe the horrors and heroism.

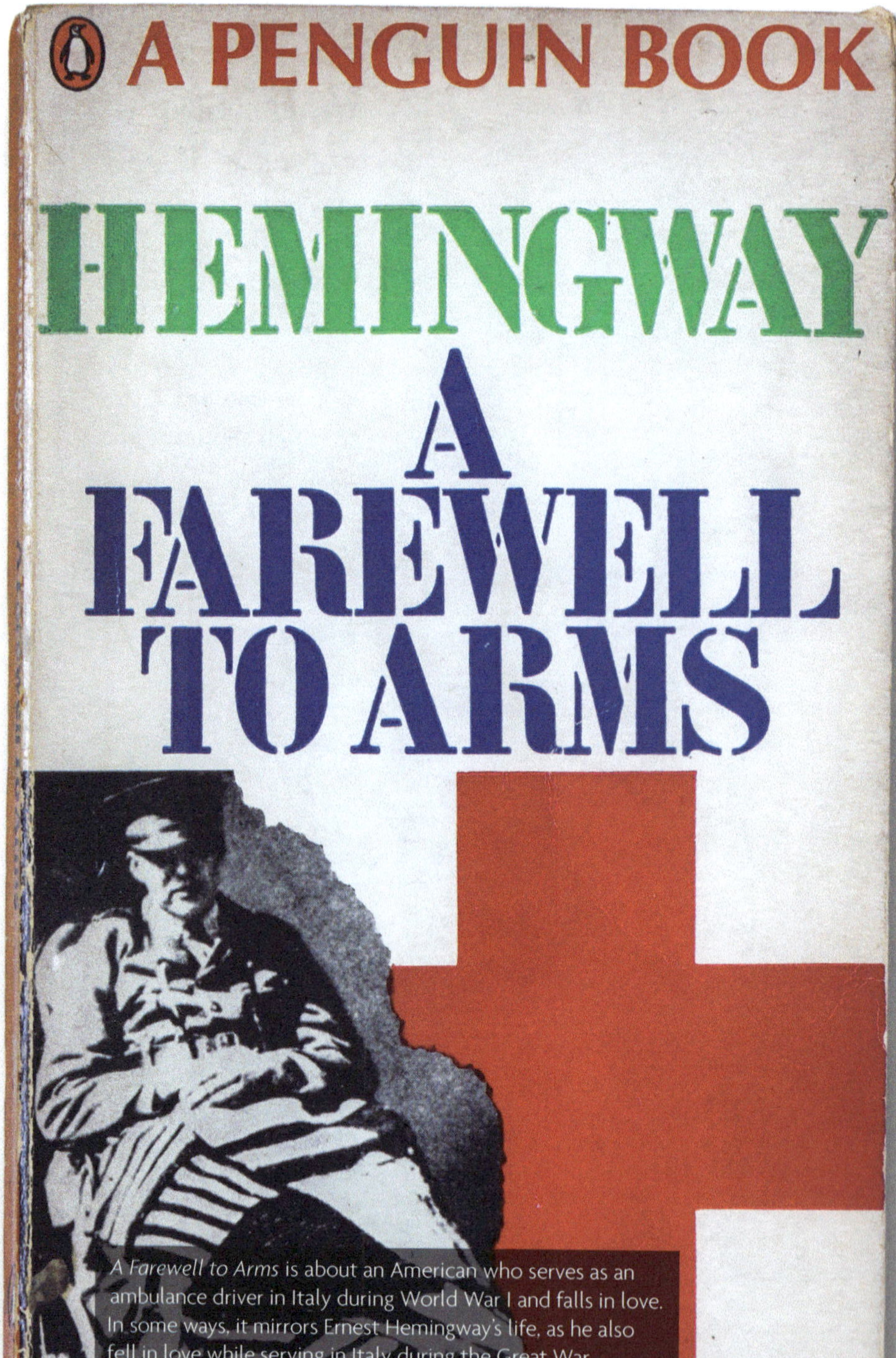

A Farewell to Arms is about an American who serves as an ambulance driver in Italy during World War I and falls in love. In some ways, it mirrors Ernest Hemingway's life, as he also fell in love while serving in Italy during the Great War.

8 World War I Writers

World War I saw an outpouring of classic writings from those who experienced it. Novels such as Erich Maria Remarque's *All Quiet on the Western Front* and Ernest Hemingway's *A Farewell to Arms* still illuminate war's effect on its participants. Poets such as Alan Seeger, Wilfred Owen, and John McCrae expressed eternal truths about war in their poetry. Some of the most vivid writing about World War I is by the correspondents who witnessed the battles firsthand and lived with the ordinary soldiers.

War Correspondents

Newspapers and press associations sent out writers to cover the action, despite the military's attempt to censor, or limit, their reporting. Some of the most famous correspondents of the war were Will Irwin, Ring Lardner,

Floyd Gibbons, Edwin L. James, John T. McCutcheon, Frazier Hunt, and Westbrook Pegler, who at twenty-three was the youngest correspondent. Women reported from the front too. Peggy Hull Deuell visited troop camps and spent several months with the infantry.

A Description of the Dead

Richard Harding Davis was probably the most famous correspondent of the war. His reports from the front kept Americans informed of what was happening on the battlefields. Davis expressed his belief in the importance of the correspondent's job when he stated, "This is a world war, and the world has the right to know, not what is going to happen next, but at least what has happened. If men died nobly, if women and children have suffered, if cities have been wrecked, the world should know that. Some men are trained to fight, and others are trained to write. The latter can tell you of what they have seen so that you can also see it."

Davis made the war real for thousands of Americans. Here is part of his description of the aftermath of a battle.

> After the Germans were repulsed at Meaux and at Sezanne the dead of both armies were so many that they lay intermingled in layers three and four deep. They were buried in long pits and piled on top of each other like cigars in a box. Lines of fresh earth so long that you mistook them for trenches intended to conceal regiments, were in reality graves. Some bodies lay for days uncovered until they lost all human semblance. They were so many you ceased to regard them even as corpses. They had become just part of the waste, a part of the shattered walls, uprooted

KEY TERMS AND CONCEPTS

From Richard Harding Davis's account:

cease To stop.

intermingle To mix together.

Meaux and Sezanne Two towns east of Paris.

repulse To drive back.

semblance Form or appearance.

From Alan Seeger's letter to the *New York Sun*:

battery A group of cannons or other artillery.

burrow A hole in the ground in which small animals, like rabbits, live.

vermin Small, harmful animals or bugs, like lice.

From Herman Warner's account:

condition To adapt or modify a response to something.

demarcation Something that marks the limit or boundary.

trees, and fields ploughed by shells. What once had been your fellow men were only bundles of clothes, swollen and shapeless, like scarecrows stuffed with rags, polluting the air.

—From Richard Harding Davis. Quoted in Steven Jantzen, *Hooray for Peace, Hurrah for War* (New York: Alfred A. Knopf, 1971).

CONSIDER THIS

1. What tone does Davis set in this selection?
2. How might the military have reacted to Davis's account? Do you think it was important for people on the home front to read it?
3. What would you have thought of the war if you had read this in America while World War I was fought abroad?

A Poet Fights for France

Alan Seeger was an American poet who served in the French Foreign Legion during World War I. Seeger was born in New York City in 1888. He studied literature at Harvard University and contributed his poetry to the *Harvard Monthly*. After graduation, Seeger moved to Paris, France, where he planned to continue his writing.

When war broke out in 1914, Seeger decided that he had to fight for freedom and for France, his adopted home. While serving in the war, Seeger found time to write numerous letters and poems. His most famous poem is "I Have a Rendezvous with Death."

The following is what Alan Seeger had to say about his experiences in the trenches. His observations appeared in letters to the *New York Sun* in the first years of the war. Seeger died on July 4, 1916, while charging a German machine-gun nest. He was twenty-eight years old.

> This style of warfare is extremely modern and for the artillerymen is doubtless very interesting, but for the poor common soldier it is anything but romantic. His role is simply to dig himself a hole in the ground and to keep hidden in it as tightly as possible. Continually under the fire of the opposing batteries, he is yet

Despite Alan Seeger's frank account in the *New York Sun*, critics say his poems about the war were a bit idealistic and romanticized.

never allowed to get a glimpse of the enemy. Exposed to the dangers of war … he is condemned to sit like an animal in its burrow and hear the shells whistle over his head and take their little daily toll from his comrades …

His feet are numb, his canteen frozen, but he is not allowed … to light a candle, but must fold himself in his blanket and lie down cramped in the dirty straw to sleep as best he may.

> Cramped quarters breed ill temper and disputes. The impossibility of the simplest kind of personal cleanliness make vermin a universal ill against which there is no remedy …
>
> Six days is the regular period for service in the trenches under normal conditions. Often enough it seems close to the limit of physical and moral strain which a man can bear. The last night the company packs up its belongings and either in the twilight of the evening or dawn assembles and waits for the shadowy arrival of the relieving sections to whom the position is surrendered without regret.
>
> —From Alan Seeger, in a letter to the *New York Sun*, December 8, 1914.

CONSIDER THIS

1. Why do you think people romanticize war? Why are accounts like Seeger's important?
2. What do you think Seeger meant by calling the warfare "modern"?
3. Why, in Seeger's opinion, was fighting an "invisible" enemy so difficult?

The Complexity of Warfare

There were also reports from those who entered the war not as Americans but ended up in the United States. Their accounts have become part of the American memory of the war.

Dr. Herman Warner was born in 1897 in Jamaica. He served in the British West Indies Forces from 1916 to 1918. He saw action on the Western Front in Belgium. This is where some of the fiercest fighting took place.

When the war ended, Warner came to the United States and settled in Harlem in New York City. He graduated from Howard University Medical School and practiced medicine in Harlem. Warner died in 1988. In this recollection, he recounts his war years.

> I saw hand-to-hand combat. You get scared. Anybody who tells you that he was not scared is a liar. There is a line of demarcation between fear and cowardice. When your buddy falls next to you, you regret it, but you're glad it wasn't you ...
>
> I came from a religious background, and at times you would feel, "What am I doing here?" Just the thought of killing a person. But then you get completely conditioned, not only to the environment but to that way of life. So many years, you were taken up with escape, just trying to get away, that you didn't have enough time to look at the individuals you were fighting. And you didn't always kill. Sometimes you would maim, and then go on about your business ... It's horrible, but it then shows you how complex a human being is.
>
> —From Jeff Kisselloff, *You Must Remember This: An Oral History of Manhattan from the 1890s to World War II* (New York: Schocken Books, 1989).

CONSIDER THIS

1. What do you think Dr. Warner meant by the statement, "There is a line of demarcation between fear and cowardice"?

2. How does he explain the apparent contradiction between being a peace-loving, gentle person and being a soldier?

"The Cathedral of Rheims"

Joyce Kilmer was born in New Brunswick, New Jersey, in 1886. He studied at Rutgers College and Columbia University. After graduation, Kilmer worked as a newspaperman for the *New York Times*. His poem "Trees" appeared in *Poetry* magazine in 1913 and won Kilmer national fame. Kilmer served in France and was killed in 1918 while attacking a German machine-gun nest.

The following excerpt is from the poem "The Cathedral of Rheims," in which Kilmer describes the medieval cathedral of Rheims, France.

He who walks through the meadows of Champagne
  At noon in Fall, when leaves like gold appear,
  Sees it draw near
Like some great mountain set upon the plain,
From radiant dawn until the close of day,
  Nearer it grows
  To him who goes
Across the country. When tall towers lay
  Their shadowy pall
  Upon his way,
  He enters, where
The solid stone is hollowed deep by all
Its centuries of beauty and prayer …

Sacred through art, from pinnacle to base:
And in thy panes of gold and scarlet glass
The setting sun sees thousandfold his face;

Sorrow and joy, in stately silence pass
Across thy walls, the shadow and the light;
Around thy lofty pillars, tapers white
Illuminate, with delicate sharp flames
The brows of saints with venerable names,
And in the night erect a fiery wall.
A great but silent fervour burns in all
Those simple folk who kneel, pathetic, dumb,
And know that down below, beside the Rhine—
Cannon, horses, soldiers, flags in line—
With blare of trumpets, mighty armies come …

Now war has come, and peace is at an end …

—From Joyce Kilmer, *Poems, Essays and Letters* (New York: George H. Doran Publishers, 1918).

CONSIDER THIS

1. To what does the poet compare the cathedral?
2. While people are praying inside, what is taking place outside the cathedral walls?
3. What comment do you think Kilmer was making about ordinary people caught up in war?
4. Why do you think Kilmer chose to write a war poem about a cathedral?

"In Flanders Fields"

John McCrae was a Canadian soldier, doctor, and poet. Although there are many poems about World War I, he wrote the most well-known one. McCrae wrote "In Flanders Fields" the day after one of his closest friends was killed in battle. The simple wooden cross that marked his friend's grave inspired McCrae to write the

KEY TERMS AND CONCEPTS

From "The Cathedral of Rheims":

fervour Fervor, or intensity.

pall Something that covers or conceals, like a drape.

pinnacle An upright structure on a building, usually ending in a spire.

Rhine A major European river that forms part of the border between France and Germany.

venerable Worthy of respect.

From " In Flanders Fields":

foe Enemy.

following lines. The poppy, a bright red flower, became the symbol of the war. It is still used to recall the dead on days of remembrance. Although this poem was not written by an American, it captures the sentiments of many about the war.

In Flanders fields the poppies blow
Between the crosses, row on row
That mark our place; and in the sky
The larks still bravely singing, fly
Scarce heard amid the guns below.

We are the Dead. Short days ago
We lived, felt dawn, saw sunset glow.

Loved, and were loved, and now we lie
In Flanders fields.

Take up our quarrel with the foe;
To you from failing hands we throw
The torch, be yours to hold it high.

If ye break faith with us who die
We shall not sleep, though poppies grow
In Flanders fields.

—John McCrae, "In Flanders Fields," 1919.

CONSIDER THIS

1. Who is the speaker in this poem?
2. What does he want?
3. What will happen if faith is broken with the dead?

The End of the War

After much devastation, peace came in November 1918. Germany surrendered. Its army could not hold out against the Allies once American troops were in the fight. American soldiers were not the only factor that brought the war to a close. Food from American farms and money from US Treasury loans helped win the war for the Allies. Some of this support was inspired by the accounts of the war like those in this chapter.

When the armistice was signed in November 1918, people flooded the streets of New York City in celebration.

9 The War to End All Wars

World War I officially ended on the eleventh hour of the eleventh day of the eleventh month of 1918. November 11 would go down in history as Armistice Day, when fighting stopped and the road to peace began. Although the formal peace treaty would not be signed until the following year, the war was over. As people began to recover from the devastation, World War I picked up the nickname "The War to End All Wars." Unfortunately, however, decisions made at the close of this war would only lead to another.

The Armistice Is Signed

The following is a description of the days that led up to the signing of the armistice.

The war came to an end on Monday, Nov. 11, 1918 at 11 o'clock a.m., French time; 6 o'clock Washington time. The armistice, which was imposed upon Germany by the Allies and the United States, was signed by the German plenipotentiaries at 5 o'clock a.m., Paris time; midnight, Washington time.

The conclusion of the armistice followed within three weeks after the dispatch of a note from the German Government to President Wilson, in which it was affirmed that a fundamental change had been made in the German Government and asking that steps be taken to arrange an armistice.

On Oct. 23 President Wilson replied by agreeing to take up with the Allies the question of an armistice. On Oct. 25 a dispatch was allowed to go from Berlin stating that an enormous crowd had assembled before the Reichstag building calling for the abdication of the Kaiser and the formation of a republic.

On Oct. 31 the representatives of the allied Governments held a formal meeting at Versailles to consider the armistice terms for Austria, which would foreshadow the terms to be submitted to Germany …

The Supreme War Council resumed its sessions at Versailles on Nov. 1 to consider the armistice terms which would be submitted to Austria and Germany …

On Nov. 3 the armistice with Austria was signed in the field. On Nov. 6, it was announced from Berlin that a German delegation to conclude an armistice and take up peace negotiations had left for the western front …

The [German] delegates crossed the allied line near La Capelle late on the night of Nov. 7. The white-flag bearers … arrived … within the French lines about 2 o'clock a.m., Nov. 8, and passed the remainder of the night there. They were taken to a house at Rethondes, six miles east of Compiegne and thirty miles from Marshal Foch's headquarters, where preparations had been made to receive them.

The automobiles conveying the delegates carried white flags and were preceded by a trumpeter. Some French soldiers under an officer approached them on the road just outside the lines.

The delegates established their identity and showed their credentials. The members of the German party were then blindfolded and the delegates proceeded to the place where they spent the night.

The delegates were received by Marshal Foch at Rethondes at 9 o'clock on the morning of Nov. 8, in a railroad car, in which the Commander in Chief of the allied force had his headquarters.

Marshal Foch then read the terms in a loud voice, dwelling upon each word. The Germans were prepared by semi-official communications for the stipulations as a whole, but hearing set forth in detail the concrete demands seemed to bring to them for the first time full realization of the extent of the German defeat.

The abdication of the Kaiser and the revolution in Germany occurred the day following the receipt of the armistice terms, Nov. 9, but no decision was announced respecting the acceptance of the armistice.

The German courier bearing the text of the armistice conditions arrived at German headquarters at 10 o'clock a.m., Nov. 10. The courier, Captain Helldorf, was long delayed while the German batteries persisted in bombarding the route he had to follow.

Nineteen hours after the German courier reached the German headquarters—at 5 o'clock a.m. Paris time, Nov. 11—the armistice was signed and the official announcement was made at Washington at 2:40 a.m., Nov. 11, by the Secretary of State. President Wilson was notified immediately by telephone.

—From staff article in *New York Times Current History*, December 1918.

CONSIDER THIS

1. Who imposed the armistice on whom?
2. When was the armistice signed?
3. Why do you think the Allies took such pains to state the terms of the armistice?

Germans Lay Down Their Arms

News of the signing of the armistice spread across the Western Front. Soldiers on both sides of the conflict knew this was the end of four long years of fighting. Here is how one American soldier, Lieutenant Walter Davenport, described what happened

KEY TERMS AND CONCEPTS

From the *New York Times Current History*:

affirm To confirm.

courier A messenger.

Marshal Foch Ferdinand Foch, head of the French forces.

plenipotentiary A diplomat with the power to negotiate on behalf of a nation.

Reichstag The primary legislative, or lawmaking, building of the German government.

stipulation A condition or a requirement.

From Walter Davenport's account:

bandoleer A belt worn across the upper body to support cartridges of ammunition.

From Kirke L. Simpson's article:

reverent Worshipful.

in the area around Saint-Mihiel, France, at eleven in the morning on November 11.

> It was 10:60 precisely and—the roar stopped like a motor car hitting a wall ... Germans began to appear ... They threw their rifles, hats, bandoleers, bayonets and trench knives toward us. They began to sing.

—From Frank Freidel, *Over There: The Story of America's First Great Overseas Crusade* (Boston: Little, Brown and Company, 1964).

CONSIDER THIS

1. What did the German soldiers do after they stopped firing? Why do you think they did this?

The Tomb of the Unknown Solider

By 1921, the United States was in the midst of a period of fun, free-spending, and fortune-building. This time in the nation's history came to be known as the Jazz Age, or the Roaring Twenties. The war and its miseries were gone but not erased from memory.

In November 1921, the remains of an unidentified American soldier were brought from a grave in France to the United States for a military funeral. The unidentified solider was buried in Arlington National Cemetery in Washington, DC, in what is known as the Tomb of the Unknown Soldier.

Kirke L. Simpson was a member of the Associated Press at the time. He wrote about the event over three days—November 9, 10, and 11. Simpson was awarded the 1922 Pulitzer Prize in Reporting for these pieces. The following is an excerpt from the third and final article.

> Under the wide and starry skies of his own homeland America's unknown dead from France sleeps tonight, a soldier home from the wars …
>
> All day long the nation poured out its heart in pride and glory for the nameless American. Before the first crash of the minute guns roared its knell for the dead from the shadow of the Washington Monument, the

people who claim him as their own were trooping out to do him honor. They lined the long road from the Capitol to the hillside where he sleeps tonight … they choked the bridges that lead across the river to the fields of the brave, in which he is the last comer.

As he was carried past through the banks of humanity that lined Pennsylvania Avenue a solemn, reverent hush held the living walls …

Out there in the broad avenue was a simple soldier, dead for honor of the flag. He was nameless. No man knew what part in the great life of the nation he had filled when last he passed over his home soil. But in France he had died as Americans always have been ready to die, for the flag and what it means …

Lifted by his hero-bearers from the stage, the unknown was carried in his flag-wrapped, simple coffin out the wide sweep of the terrace. The bearers laid the sleeper down above the crypt, on which had been placed a little of the soil of France …

A rocking blast of gunfire rang from the woods. The glittering circle of bayonets stiffened to a salute to the dead …

The guns roared out again in the national salute. He was home, The Unknown, to sleep forever among his own.

—From Kirke L. Simpson, "America's Unknown Dead from France Sleeps Tonight," 1921.

CONSIDER THIS

1. How did the American people react to the burying of the soldier?
2. Why would the nation honor a soldier whose name nobody knows?

A Fourteen-Point Plan

Although Americans honored those who fought, they were eager to put the war and complications in Europe behind them. They felt this way even before the end of the war. President Woodrow Wilson, however, felt the need for an international organization in order to achieve greater peace.

Even before the fighting stopped, President Wilson called for a plan that would address the problems that had led to war in the first place. The plan was called the Fourteen Points. He outlined the plan for Congress in January 1918. Wilson's goal was not only to end World War I but to prevent future wars.

> What we demand in this war … is that the world be made fit and safe to live in; and particularly that it be made safe for every peace-loving nation … The program of the world's peace, therefore, is our program; and that program … as we see it, is this:
>
> I. Open covenants of peace, openly arrived at, after which there shall be no private international understandings of any kind but diplomacy shall proceed always frankly and in the public view.
>
> II. Absolute freedom of navigation upon the seas, outside territorial waters, alike in peace and in war …

Wilson's Fourteen Points mostly fell on deaf ears in Congress in 1918; however, he accurately predicted the dangers of isolationism.

III. The removal, so far as possible, of all economic barriers and the establishment of an equality of trade conditions among all the nations consenting to the peace …

IV. Adequate guarantees given and taken that national armaments will be reduced to the lowest point consistent with domestic safety.

V. A free, open-minded, and absolutely impartial adjustment of all colonial claims ...

VI. The evacuation of all Russian territory and such settlement of all questions affecting Russia as will secure ... for her ... an opportunity for the independent determination of her own political development ...

VII. Belgium ... must be evacuated and restored ...

VIII. All French territory should be freed and the invaded portions restored ...

IX. A readjustment of the frontiers of Italy ... along clearly recognizable lines of nationality.

X. The peoples of Austria-Hungary ... should be accorded the freest opportunity of autonomous development.

XI. Rumania, Serbia, and Montenegro should be evacuated; occupied territories restored; Serbia accorded free and secure access to the sea; and the relations of the several Balkan states to one another determined by friendly counsel along historically established lines of allegiance and nationality ...

XII. The Turkish portions of the present Ottoman Empire should be assured a secure sovereignty ... and the Dardanelles should be permanently opened as a free passage to the ships and commerce of all nations under international guarantees.

KEY TERMS AND CONCEPTS

From Woodrow Wilson's Fourteen Points:

accord To grant.

armament Armed forces or weapons.

autonomous Having the right to self-govern.

covenant A binding agreement.

diplomacy The skillful handling of affairs between nations.

impartial Not biased.

sovereignty A supreme power, or freedom to be an independent country.

territorial integrity An agreement to honor a country's borders.

From Woodrow Wilson's warning:

deplore To express strong disapproval.

evident Obvious.

exaltation A feeling of extreme happiness.

exhibition Display.

prevail To be victorious.

render To give or make.

XIII. An independent Polish state should be erected ...

XIV. A general association of nations must be formed ... for the purpose of affording mutual guarantees of political independence and territorial integrity to great and small states alike.

We have no jealousy of German greatness ... We do not wish to injure her or to block in any way her legitimate influence of power. We do not wish to fight her either with arms or with hostile arrangements of trade if she is willing to associate herself with us and the other peace-loving nations of the world in covenants of justice and law and fair dealing.

—From Congressional Record: Vol. LVI, 1918, pt. I: pp. 680–681.

CONSIDER THIS

1. What are some of the key words Wilson used in this document?
2. What did Wilson hope to achieve in point fourteen?
3. How do you think members of the various countries he mentioned felt about this plan?

Wilson's Legacy and Warning

Wilson, ultimately, was unable to convince Congress of his plan. The fourteenth point was his push for the League of Nations. However, his explanation did not convince Congress to support it. He took part in the Versailles peace conference in 1919. While there, he insisted that the delegates establish the Covenant, which was the constitution of the League of Nations. Yet Wilson could do nothing to stop the Allies from placing harsh penalties on Germany and the Central powers.

Unlike Wilson, the rest of the Allies were more interested in punishing Germany. The final peace agreement, the Treaty of Versailles, stripped Germany of many of its colonies, limited its military, and required the country to pay war reparations, or payment for damages. The peace conference in Versailles did, however, create the League of Nations. This organization was the type of general association Wilson hoped for in his fourteenth point.

Although the Allies supported the League of Nation, Wilson was unable to convince Congress to support it or the Treaty of Versailles, which he helped draft. When the time came for the Senate to ratify, or approve, the peace treaty, it refused to do so. The United States didn't join the League of Nations. Most Americans didn't understand why the country should join this organization in the first place.

For Wilson, the end of the war brought only personal defeat. On top of his inability to convince Congress to play a role in international peacekeeping, Wilson suffered a devastating stroke that left him in ill health. He did not run for reelection as the Democratic candidate in 1920. However, the candidate from his political party pledged to take the United States into the League. The election outcome proved that Americans wanted to forget the war. Voters chose Republican Warren G. Harding, who promised "a return to normalcy," as their new president.

Three years later, on November 10, 1923, Wilson gave a speech on the radio in honor of Armistice Day. He reminded Americans of what they had won in the Great War. He urged listeners to continue taking part in the affairs of the world. He thought international involvement was important for the peace and democracy American soldiers had died to preserve. The following is an excerpt from that speech.

The anniversary of Armistice Day should stir us to great exaltation of spirit because of the proud recollection that it was our day ... which lifted the world to the high levels of vision and achievement upon which the great war for democracy and right was fought and won ... When the victory was won ... we turned our backs upon our associates [the Allies] and refused to bear any responsible part in the administration of peace ... and withdrew into a sullen and selfish isolation ...

That we should have thus done a great wrong to civilization at one of the most critical turning points in the history of the world is the more to be deplored because every anxious year that has followed has made the need for such services as we might have rendered more and more evident and more and more pressing ...

The affairs of the world can be set straight only by the firmest and most determined exhibition of the will to lead and make the right prevail.

—From Woodrow Wilson's radio address, November 10, 1923.

CONSIDER THIS

1. Why did Wilson disapprove of America's actions after World War I?
2. What do you think he meant by the "will to lead"?

The End of One War

Wilson was right when it came to needing to continue to be aware of the events of the world. In the twentieth century, Americans would discover just how interconnected all of the nations were. One decade after the end of World War I, the United States would fall into a terrible economic depression that would have international consequences. On the heels of this devastation would come another world war.

In the post–World War I period, the former Allies showed no will to correct the ills that had led to the Great War. They also were unable to anticipate and deal with aggressive actions by Germany, Japan, and Italy. Across the Atlantic, Americans could little understand the deeply felt national hatreds that would produce World War II. The War to End All Wars had not lived up to its name.

CHRONOLOGY

1914 Archduke Franz Ferdinand is assassinated in Bosnia by a Serb. War is declared between the Allies (France, Great Britain, and Russia) and the Central Powers (Germany, Austria-Hungary, and the Ottoman Empire). The First Battle of the Marne occurs. The first trenches are dug along the Western Front. The First Battle of Ypres occurs.

1915 Germany begins its submarine blockade of Great Britain. Germans launch the first attack of poisonous gas, targeting French-Algerian troops in Belgium. A German submarine torpedoes and sinks the British passenger liner *Lusitania*. Italy enters the war on the side of the Allies.

1916 Germans attack the French city of Verdun, and the battle continues for ten months. The Battle of Jutland in the North Sea, one of the largest sea battles ever, occurs. The British, with French help, begin a large-scale attack along the Somme River in northwest France. The British introduce the use of the tank. Woodrow Wilson is elected for a second term.

1917 German submarines begin unrestricted warfare in British waters. The US declares war on Germany. The

Selective Service Act becomes law. The first US troops reach France. Russia signs an armistice with Germany; fighting on the Eastern Front ends.

1918 President Wilson announces the Fourteen Points, his plan for peace. Influenza breaks out at an army camp in Kansas, the first outbreak in the United States; by fall, the disease will have become an international crisis. The Germans launch the first of five major offensives on the Western Front and push back the Allies. The German offensive is then halted. The battle between US and German troops at Château-Thierry in France ends in a US victory. General Pershing takes command of US troops at Saint-Mihiel, occupied by Germans since the beginning of the war. American infantry break through German lines on the first day of the Saint-Mihiel offensive, defeating the enemy in four days. The Meuse-Argonne offensive begins, the goal of which is to push the Germans out of France. The Germans dispatch a cable to President Wilson, asking for peace. Kaiser Wilhelm II abdicates and flees Germany. The Central Powers surrender. The armistice is signed, and fighting ends on the Western Front. The war is over.

1919 The peace conference opens in Versailles, France. It leads to the Treaty of Versailles, which is signed in Paris. President Wilson sends the Treaty of Versailles and the Covenant of the League of Nations to the Senate for ratification; he declares that acceptance of the treaty would ensure world peace. The Senate refuses to ratify the Treaty of Versailles, and the United States does not join the League of Nations.

GLOSSARY

abdicate To give up the throne.

annex To incorporate a territory into a country or a nation state.

blockade The act of sealing off a space in order to prevent goods or people from entering or exiting.

conscription Forced enrollment into the armed forces.

cruiser A large, fast warship outfitted with guns.

doughboy The name for an American soldier during World War I.

isolationism The belief that a nation should stay out of international politics or affairs.

kaiser The ruler or emperor of Germany.

mobilize To prepare for war.

no-man's-land The space between two enemy trenches.

Ottoman Empire Also known as the Turkish Empire, a group of nations that included much of Asia Minor and southeastern Europe that existed under one authority from the thirteenth century until it collapsed after World War I.

pacifist A person who believes peace should be maintained at any cost.

shell shock The state of being worn out or mentally exhausted by the stress of battle. Today, the condition is known as post-traumatic stress disorder (PTSD).

shrapnel Fragments from an explosive shell filled with lead balls that explodes in midair, scattering the lead balls.

sniper A person shooting from a hiding place.

stalemate A point at which neither side in a conflict can take action.

U-boat A short name for a German submarine.

ultimatum A final demand or condition.

FURTHER INFORMATION

BOOKS

Atwood, Kathryn J. *Women Heroes of World War I: 16 Remarkable Resisters, Soldiers, Spies, and Medics*. Women of Action. Chicago, IL: Chicago Review Press, 2014.

Hemingway, Ernest. *A Farewell to Arms*. New York, NY: Scribner, 2014.

Remarque, Erich Maria. *All Quiet on the Western Front*. Everyman's Library. New York, NY: Knopf, 2018.

World War I and the Rise of Global Conflict. World History. New York, NY: Greenhaven Publishing, 2017.

WEBSITES

World War One

https://www.bl.uk/world-war-one

The British Library holds over five hundred sources from across Europe surrounding World War I.

World War I Centennial
https://www.si.edu/spotlight/wwi100

The Smithsonian Institution commemorated the one hundredth anniversary of the US involvement in the war through its museums, archives, libraries, and exhibitions. The commemoration is archived on this website.

World War I: War of Images, Images of War
http://www.getty.edu/research/exhibitions_events/exhibitions/ww1/

This Getty Research Institute website provides an archive of an exhibition focused on war propaganda and depictions of war by artists who witnessed it.

VIDEOS

Europe Prior to World War I: Alliances and Enemies
https://www.youtube.com/watch?v=f11CKYB2FCA

This three-part video series, starting with the video above, explains some events in Europe that led to World War I.

The Harlem Hellfighters
https://www.youtube.com/watch?v=eEuoAl1elLU

This video provides a brief overview of the Harlem Hellfighters and the difficulties these black soldiers faced in the United States.

ORGANIZATIONS

Library of Congress
101 Independence Ave., SE
Washington, DC 20540
(202) 707-5000

Website: https://www.loc.gov

The Library of Congress holds primary-source materials, such as newspapers and articles, about World War I.

National Archives
700 Pennsylvania Ave., NW
Washington, DC 20408
(866) 272-6272

Website: https://www.archives.gov

The National Archives maintain the country's records, such as military records related to those who served in the Great War.

National WWI Museum and Memorial
2 Memorial Drive
Kansas City, MO 64108
(816) 888-8100

Website: https://www.theworldwar.org

This institution is dedicated to providing context for World War I and its global impact while also maintaining the Liberty Memorial, which honors those who served in the war.

Office of the Historian
US Department of State
Washington, DC
(202) 955-0200

Website: http://history.state.gov

This office in the US State Department is responsible for gathering and distributing information about US foreign policy, in addition to answering questions related to US history.

United Nations
405 East 42nd Street
New York, NY 10017
(212) 963-1234

Website: https://www.un.org/en

This organization replaced the League of Nation, which failed to prevent World War II.

INDEX

Page numbers in **boldface** refer to images.

ABOUT THE AUTHORS

Chet'la Sebree is a writer, editor, and researcher from the Mid-Atlantic. She has received degrees in English and writing from the University of Richmond and American University, respectively. She has worked on several books about US history, including the Courting History series for Cavendish Square Publishing. Her research focus is early American history.

Adriane Ruggiero writes frequently about history, both ancient and modern, and international affairs. Specifically, she's written about eastern European nations, empires, the Middle Ages, and ancient Greece and Rome. She's also written substantially on military history. She resides in Teaneck, New Jersey.